TOP 20 BUSINESS STRATEGIES

FOR BUSINESS GROWTH

by

Shabbar Suterwala

Pick up any Strategy and directly apply it in your Business within Minutes.

Authored & Published by

Shabbar Suterwala

Address

B/303, Mandsaur Co-op. Hsg., Soc.
Kokani Pada, Kurar Village, Malad (East)
Mumbai 400097
INDIA

Email: ShabbarSuterwala@gmail.com

www.ShabbarSuterwala.com

Copyright 2019

Preface

As a Soft Skills Trainer and a Business Coach for more than 20 years now, I discovered that small and medium size business owners keep on doing the business the way they have done it for years. There is a Mindset that Business Strategies are only for Corporates. Many businessmen did not get an opportunity to be at B-Schools. They are self-made with their hard-work and learning from their mistakes and past experiences.

Such Businessmen have a great Motivation level and the Right Attitude, what is missing though is the right Knowledge about Business Strategies that will help them build and leverage their Business and take it to the next level.

This book on **"Top 20 Business Strategies for Business Growth"** is a unique hand book for such small and medium size businessmen who simply read a few pages of any strategy and apply it into their Business and immediately see the results.

Out of the numerous business strategies freely available today over the internet which run into millions of pages, I have hand-picked 20 Business Strategies that will help the businessmen to plan, organize, secure a strong competitive market position which will lead to strong financial performance and thus grow their business to the next level.

I have done a thorough reading, research on the strategies and my sincere acknowledgement to all the people or authors or owners who have derived the respective strategy. There are numerous books on each strategy and the internet is flooded with resources on each strategy. The objective of this book is to introduce you to the top 20 business strategies for your business growth with the introduction, simple explanation and understanding, examples and illustrations that will help you to apply the strategy into your business within minutes.

You can read all the strategies at one go or can pick up one strategy at a time, read it, understand it and apply in your business and get the results and then move to another.

There is an Action Plan chart on the last page of this book, that will help you to plan and take action on each strategy

Wishing you a Happy Reading and Lots of Learning.

Shabbar Suterwala (Spreading the Smiles)

Date: 31st March, 2019

TABLE OF CONTENTS

--*-*-*

"A VISION WITHOUT A STRATEGY

IS AN ILLUSION."

LEE BOLMAN

--*-*-*

Business Strategy No.1
SWOT ANALYSIS

Introduction:

SWOT Analysis is an acronym for Strengths, Weaknesses, Opportunities, and Threats and is a structured planning method that evaluates four elements of an organization, project or **business** venture.

SWOT Analysis is a simple but useful framework to help you Focus on your Strengths, Minimize Threats, and take the greatest possible advantage of Opportunities available to you.

A **SWOT analysis** can be carried out for a **company**, product, place, industry, or person.

The Strengths & Weaknesses relate to the Present Business Situation and the Opportunities & Threats relate to the Future of the Business. Strengths and Weaknesses are often internal to your organization, while opportunities and threats generally relate to external factors. Also, Strengths & Opportunities are the Positive & Weaknesses & Threats are the Negative side of your Business.

This assessment technique has a remarkable track record of success, providing almost accurate and extremely helpful insights to businesses. To help you understand better how it works, let's look at some SWOT Analysis examples.

Example 1: SWOT Analysis:

Strengths
- Have an excellent staff for handling sales with strong knowledge of current products
- Strong customer relationships
- Strong internal communications system
- A strong geographical location with high traffic input
- Well-designed and successful marketing strategies
- Business reputation of being innovative

Weaknesses
- Too many missed deadlines and a lot of work on pending
- High cost of rental for the office
- Infrequent cash flow system
- Too much stock in inventory and higher inventory costs
- An inefficient record maintenance system in place
- Outdated market research data

Opportunities
- Products similar to yours in the market are expensive or of poor quality
- Customers in the market are loyal
- Seasonal high demand of the product
- High demand for product or similar merchandise

Threats
- A lot of competitors in the market with similar products
- A new advertising campaign launched by competitors
- A competitor opening new shop in a nearby location

- A downturn in economy and less spending budget of people

Example 2: SWOT Analysis (Small Firm or Company)

Strengths
- We are able to respond very quickly as we have no Hierarchy in Organization Structure
- We are able to give really good customer care as we are small
- Bosses have a strong reputation in the market.
- Loyal Staff working since the organization started
- We can change quickly if we find that something is not working.
- We have low overheads & less advertising, so we can offer good value to customers

Weaknesses
- Our company has little market presence and that too only locally
- We have a small number of staff and that too untrained
- Knowledge and Skills of the Staff not at par with the Current Market Growth
- Challenges when Staff is Sick or go on Leave
- Cash flow problems at time due to Credit
- Limited amount of Inventory due to Customer demand Variety

Opportunities
- Expansion in terms of Products & Service

- Increase in Growth and Profit if we expand / Branches
- Easy Referral & Repeat Business from Happy Customers
- Competitors may have difficulty is local penetration
- Bulk & Economy Purchases if in Cash / Bosses Reputation

Threats
- Growing Technology and Online Market
- Large Organization may wipe our Market due to Volume
- Risk of Bad Debts due to Credit

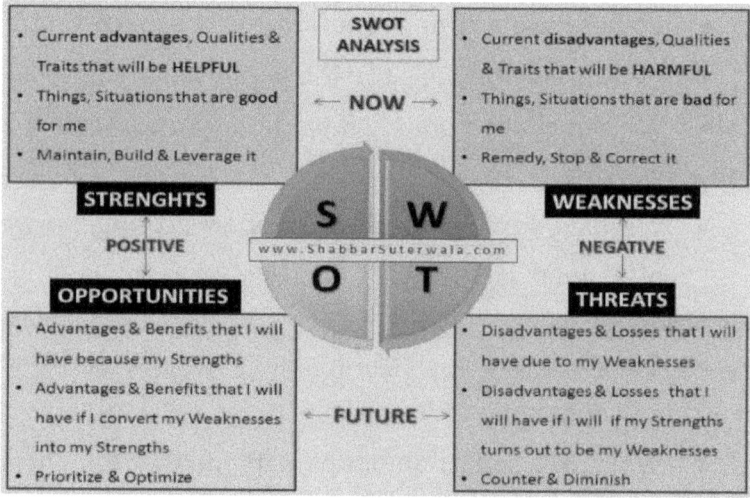

How to prepare the SWOT Analysis?

1. Use the Template on the following Page.
2. Gather Your Partners, Team and Staff together.
3. Brainstorming ideas to fill each Matrix of the SWOT analysis.
   ...
4. Determine Strengths and Weaknesses. ...
5. Identify Opportunities and Threats. ...
6. Then again do the Analysis
7. Write an Action Plan on How to Convert Weaknesses into Strength an Overcome Threats.
8. How can you tap on your Strengths and Make the Best of the Opportunities available?

S	W
O	T

SWOT ANAYSIS MATRIX

Exercise:
Take a Blank Sheet of Paper & Make the Matrix of SWOT & Answer the Questions.

Strengths:

- What do you do well?
- What unique resources can you draw on?
- What do others see as your strengths?
- What advantages does your organization have?
- What do you do better than anyone else?
- What unique or lowest-cost resources can you draw upon that others can't?
- What do people in your market see as your strengths?
- What factors mean that you "get the sale"?
- What is your organization's USP?

Weaknesses:

- What could you improve?
- Where do you have fewer resources than others?
- What are others likely to see as weaknesses?
- What could you improve?
- What should you avoid?
- What are people in your market likely to see as weaknesses?
- What are your competitors doing any better than you?
- What factors lose your sales?

Opportunities:	Threats:
<ul><li>What opportunities are open to you?</li><li>What trends could you take advantage of?</li><li>How can you turn your strengths into opportunities?</li><li>What good opportunities can you spot?</li><li>What interesting trends are you aware of?</li><li>Useful opportunities can come from such things as:</li><li>Changes in technology and markets on both a broad and narrow scale.</li><li>Changes in government policy related to your field.</li><li>Changes in social patterns, population profiles, lifestyle changes, and so on.</li><li>Local events.</li><li>Look at your strengths and ask whether these open up any opportunities.</li></ul>	<ul><li>What threats could harm you?</li><li>What is your competition doing that you are not?</li><li>What threats do your weaknesses expose you to?</li><li>What obstacles do you face?</li><li>Are quality standards or specifications for your job, products or services are changing?</li><li>Is changing technology threatening your position?</li><li>Do you have bad debt or cash-flow problems?</li><li>Could any of your weaknesses seriously threaten your business?</li></ul>

• Look at your weaknesses and ask whether you could open up opportunities by eliminating them.	

Some Points to Note while doing the SWOT

- When looking at opportunities and threats, ensure that you don't overlook external factors, such as new government regulations, or technological changes in your industry.

- There is no point listing an opportunity (O) if the same opportunity is available to competitors.

- It is pointless to say you have strengths (S) if your competitors have the same.

- The Analysis should distinguish between where your organization is today, and where it could be in the future.

STRENGTH	WEAKNESS
Good Now	Bad Now
Maintain, Build & Leverage it	Remedy, Stop & Correct it
Build on your STRENGTHS	*Recognize your WEAKNESSES*
OPPORTUNITY	**THREAT**
Future is Good	Future is Bad
Prioritize & Optimize	Counter & Diminish
Evaluate your OPPORTUNITIES	*Research your THREATS*

Business Strategy No. 2
THE MCKINSEY 7-S FRAMEWORK

Introduction:

The McKinsey 7-S Framework is a management model developed by well-known business consultants **Robert H. Waterman**, Jr. and **Tom Peters** (who also developed the MBWA- - "Management by Walking Around" and authored the best-selling Business Book - **In Search of Excellence**) in the 1980s.

The basic premise of the model is, "for any Organization to be Successful there are seven internal aspects that needs to be aligned".

Where can the 7-S Model be used?

The 7-S model can be used in a wide variety of situations like:

- Improve the performance of a company.
- Examine the likely effects of future changes within a company.
- Align departments and processes during a change or merger or acquisition.
- Determine how best to implement a proposed strategy.
- The model is most often used as an organizational analysis tool to assess and monitor changes in the internal situation of an organization.

- This model can be applied to elements of a team or a project as well.

What are the Seven Elements?

Hard Elements - "Hard" elements are easier to define or identify and management can directly influence them: These are strategy statements; organization charts and reporting lines; and formal processes and IT systems.

- **Strategy** – The plan devised to maintain and build competitive advantage over the competition. Key approaches to achieving the Organization Goal.
- **Structure** – The way the organization is structured and who reports to whom.
- **Systems** – The daily activities and procedures that staff members engage in to get the job done. Business processes and the technical platforms used to support operations.

Soft Elements - "Soft" elements, on the other hand, can be more difficult to describe, and are less tangible and more influenced by culture. However, these soft elements are as important as the hard elements if the organization is going to be successful.

- **Skills** - the actual skills and competencies of the employees working for the company.
- **Staff** - The employees and their general capabilities in terms of educational and attitudinal characteristics.

Remuneration Package and how they are attracted and retained.

- **Style** – The Leadership Style & the culture of the organization in terms interactions between staff and other stakeholders. Typical behaviour patterns of key groups, such as bosses, managers and professionals at the top level.
- **Shared Values** – The "superordinate goals" when the model was first developed, these are the core values of the company that are evidenced in the corporate culture and the general work ethic.

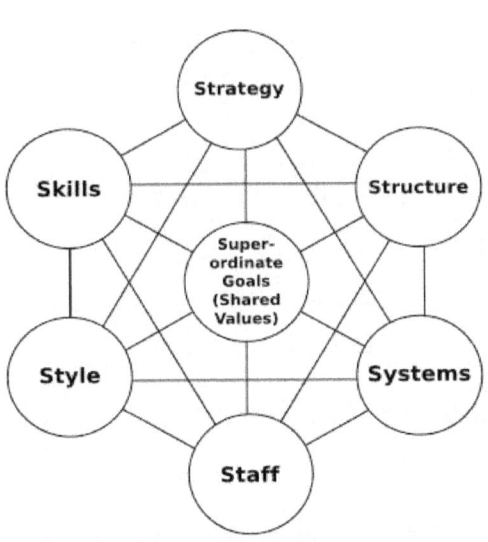

Placing Shared Values in the middle of the model emphasizes that these values are central to the development of all the other critical elements. The company's structure, strategy, systems, style, staff and skills all stem from why the organization was originally created, and what it stands for. The original vision of the company was formed from the values of the creators. As the values change, so do all the other elements.

An example of applying the 7-S Framework:

You can review each of the 7-S to assess how the capabilities of an organization can be improved as the starting point of creating an action plan.

This example considers some of the issues related to introducing digital technology into an organization.

1. **Strategy** - The contribution of digital business in influencing and supporting organization's strategy. The key issues are:

- Gaining appropriate budgets and demonstrating, delivering value and ROI from budgets.
- Annual planning approach.
- Techniques for using digital business to impact organization strategy.
- Techniques for aligning digital business strategy with organizational and marketing strategy.

2. **Structure** - The modification of organizational structure to support digital business. The key issues are:

- Integration of digital marketing or e-commerce teams with other management, marketing (corporate communications, brand marketing, direct marketing) and IT staff.

- Use of cross-functional teams.
- Insourcing v/s outsourcing.

3. **Systems** - The development of specific processes, procedures or information systems to support digital business. The key issues are:

- Planning, approach & integration.
- Managing or sharing customer information.
- Managing customer experience, service and content quality.

4. **Skills** - Distinctive capabilities of key staff, but can be interpreted as specific skill-sets of team members. The key issues are:

- staff skills in specific areas such as supplier selection,
- project management,
- content management and
- specific e-marketing media channels.

5. **Staff** - The breakdown of staff in terms of their background, age and sex and characteristics such as IT v/s marketing, use of contractors/ consultants. The key issues are:

- Insourcing v/s outsourcing.
- Achieving senior management buy-in/involvement with digital marketing.
- Staff recruitment and retention, and virtual working.

- Staff development and training.

6. **Style** - Includes both the way in which key managers behave in achieving the organization's goals and the cultural style of the organization as a whole. The key issues are:

- Defining a long-term vision for transformation. (Aadhar Card)
- Relates to role of the digital marketing or e-commerce teams in influencing strategy – is it dynamic and influential or a service which is conservative and looking for a voice.

7. **Shared values** - The guiding concepts of the digital business or e-commerce organization which are also part of shared values and culture. The key issues are:

- improving the perception of the importance and effectiveness of digital business amongst bosses & senior managers and staff it works with (marketing generalists and IT).

Remember to manage the hard and soft factors separately:

- Hard factors: Strategy, Structure and Systems.
- Soft factors: Style, Staff, Skills, Systems and Shared values/superordinate goals.

Action Plan for 7-S (Checklist of Questions)

Here are some of the questions that you'll need to explore to help you understand your situation in terms of the 7-S framework.

1. **Strategy:**
   - What is our strategy?
   - How do we intend to achieve our objectives / goals?
   - How do we deal with competitive pressure?
   - How are changes in customer demands dealt with?
   - What is plan or back up for financial impact?

2. **Structure:**
   - How is the company/team divided?
   - What is the hierarchy?
   - How do the various departments coordinate activities?
   - How do the team members organize and align themselves?
   - Is decision making and controlling centralized or decentralized?
   - Is this as it should be, given what we're doing?
   - Where are the lines of communication? Explicit and implicit?

3. **Systems:**
   - What are the main systems that run the organization? - Consider Financial and HR systems as well as Communications and document storage.
   - Where are the controls and how are they monitored and evaluated?
   - What internal rules and processes does the team use to keep on track?
   - What are the fundamental values that the company/team was built on?

4. **Skills:**
   - What are the strongest skills represented within the company/team?
   - Are there any skills gaps?
   - What is the company/team known for doing well?
   - Do the current employees/team members have the ability to do the job?
   - How are skills monitored and assessed?

5. **Style:**
   - What is the level of Trust & Influence of Leadership?
   - Is there a conflict of power at the top? Or Role Duplication?
   - How participative is the management/leadership style?

- How effective is that leadership?
- Do employees/team members tend to be competitive or cooperative?
- Are there real teams functioning within the organization or are they just nominal groups?

6. **Staff:**
   - What positions or specializations are represented within the team?
   - What positions need to be filled?
   - Are there gaps in required competencies?

7. **Shared Values:**
   - What are the core values?
   - What is the corporate/team culture?
   - How strong are the values?

--*-*-*

**"SUCCESS IS 20% SKILLS AND 80%
STRATEGY. YOU MIGHT KNOW HOW
TO SUCCEED, BUT MORE
IMPORTANTLY, WHAT'S YOUR PLAN
TO SUCCEED?"**

JIM ROHN

--*-*-*

Business Strategy No. 3
THE 5-WHY's ANALYSIS

Introduction:

The 5-Why analysis method is used to move past symptoms and understand the true root cause of a problem. so that you can deal with it once and for all.

The 5 Whys strategy is a simple, effective tool for uncovering the root of a problem. You can use it in troubleshooting, problem solving and quality improvement initiatives.

Start with a problem and ask "why" it is occurring. Make sure that your answer is grounded in fact, then ask "why" again. Continue the process until you reach the problem's root cause, and you can identify a counter-measure that prevents it from recurring.

Bear in mind that this questioning process is best suited to simple to moderately-difficult problems.

Historical Perspective

Although the 5-Why problem-solving technique has been popularized by the Japanese, this common-sense concept has been around for quite some time:

Benjamin Franklin's 5-Why Analysis:

For want of a nail a shoe was lost,
for want of a shoe a horse was lost,
for want of a horse a rider was lost,
for want of a rider an army was lost,
for want of an army a battle was lost,
for want of a battle the war was lost,
for want of the war the kingdom was lost,
and all for the want of a little horseshoe nail.

The 5-Why technique is true to this tradition, and it is most effective when the answers come from people who have hands-on experience of the process being examined. It is remarkably simple: when a problem occurs, you drill down to its root cause by asking "why?" five times. Then, when a counter-measure becomes apparent, you follow it through to prevent the issue from recurring.

When to Use the 5 Whys?

You can use 5 Whys for troubleshooting, quality improvement and problem solving, but it is most effective when used to resolve simple or moderately difficult problems.

This simple technique, however, can often direct you quickly to the root(s) of a problem. So, whenever a system or process isn't working properly, give it a try before you embark on a more in-depth approach – and certainly before you attempt to develop a solution.

How to Use 5 Whys?

The model follows a very simple process:

Step 1. Assemble a Team

Gather together people who are familiar with the detail of the problem and with the process that you're trying to fix.

Step 2. Define the Problem

If you can, observe the problem in action. Discuss it with your team and write a brief, clear problem statement that you all agree on. For example, "Marketing Team isn't meeting its targets" or "CRM Software has failures."

Then, write your statement on a whiteboard, leaving enough space around it to write your answers to the repeated question, "Why?"

Step 3. Ask the First "Why?"

Ask your team why the problem is occurring. (For example, "Why isn't marketing team meeting its targets?")

Asking "why?" sounds simple, but answering it requires thought and intelligent application. Search for answers that are grounded in fact: they must be accounts of things that have actually happened – not guesses at what might have happened.

This prevents 5 Whys from becoming just a process of deductive reasoning, which can generate a large number of possible causes and, sometimes, create more confusion as you chase down hypothetical problems. Your team members may come up with one obvious reason why, or several plausible ones. Record their answers under (or to the right of) your problem statement as phrases, rather than single words or lengthy statements.

For example, saying "volume of calls is too high" is better than a vague "overloaded "

Step 4. Ask "Why?" Four More Times

Working sequentially along one of the answers you generated in Step 3, ask four further "whys" in succession. Frame the question each time in response to the answer you've just recorded, and again record your responses to the right.

"Marketing Team isn't meeting its targets"

WHY?

"Existing Customer is not Happy"

WHY?

"Because we did not deliver on time"

WHY?

"Production / Operations took much longer than we thought"

WHY?

"We did not list / estimate the operations stages"

WHY?

"We were running behind other stuff and did not give enough attention to time estimates"

Root Cause is Time Management (Distinguishing between Urgent & Important)

Step 5. Know When to Stop

You'll have revealed the nature of the root cause when asking "why" produces no more useful responses and you can go no further. An appropriate counter-measure or process change should then become evident.

Step 6. Address the Root Cause(s)

Now that you've identified at least one true root cause, you need to discuss and agree what counter-measures will prevent the problem from recurring.

Step 7. Monitor Your Measures

Keep a close watch on how effectively your counter-measures eliminate or minimize the initial problem. You may need to amend them, or replace them with something different. If this happens, it would be sensible to repeat the 5-Whys process to ensure that you've identified the correct root cause.

Simple Example 1:

"Caught up Speeding"

WHY?

"Late for Work"

WHY?

"Got Up Late in the Morning"

WHY?

"Alarm did not Ring"

WHY?

"The Mobile Battery was Down"

WHY?

"Forgot to Keep on Charging"

Root Cause & Action Plan: Mobile Battery Recharge / No Alarm Clock / Power Bank / Laziness /

Simple Example 2:

Computers are breaking down so often that work is delayed

WHY?

The Computers are very old and software in not compatible

WHY?

Purchased almost 5 years ago

WHY?

Budget is Limited

WHY?

Manager has not made an effective presentation

WHY?

Manager in-charge is a family member and has newly joined the organization and does not have management skills.

--*-*-*

"ONLY THOSE WHO WILL RISK

GOING TOO FAR CAN POSSIBLY FIND

OUT HOW FAR ONE CAN GO"

T. S. ELIOT

--*-*-*

Business Strategy No. 4
THE 10-10-10 RULE TO MAKE DECSIONS

Introduction:

You have to make some difficult decisions through the course of your life. Business writer and author Suzy Welch suggests making that call by using the **10-10-10 rule** to get your priorities in order first.

In her book 10-10-10: A Fast and Powerful Way to Get Unstuck in Love, at Work, and with Your Family, Welch writes: *"Every time I find myself in a situation where there appears to be no solution that will make everyone happy, I ask myself three questions"*

- *What are the consequences of my decision in 10 minutes?*
- *In 10 months?*
- *And in 10 years?*

The 10-10-10 rule is simple: **How is what you're about to do going to matter in 10 minutes, 10 months or 10 years?** By asking herself three easy—and utterly profound—questions,

Suzy Welch has managed to solve just about every personal and professional quandary in her life and have made some tough decisions in her Life. The way the brain works, your decisions are rooted in feelings , and the long-term considerations should help in making those clear. Welch says that with the answers, you will figure out if the decision is aligned with your priorities, or maybe even discover your priorities in the process. The clarity of thought also makes it easy to explain the choice to those who will feel its impact.

Let's Understand the 10-10-10 with a very Simple Example:

Raju is a smart boy, quiet, introvert with a dry sense of humor and a generous spirit. He's 20 years young, a college student and has never been very good at talking to women.

One day, a girl that he has liked for months sits next to him in his science class. He is nervous, but knows that he needs to summon the courage to talk to women he likes one of these days.

Then, by a stroke of luck, the professor assigns the two of them to work on a project together. He starts building a friendship with her. He is awkward at times, but they generally get along well.

After a week of working together, they exchange phone numbers so that they can collaborate on the project better.

With her number in hand, Raju wants to call her and ask her out on a cup of coffee & movie, but he is incredibly scared.

Raju runs through every possible scenario in his head.

- *What if he messes up and sounds weird on the phone?*
- *What if she says "no"? The rest of the project is going to be extremely awkward!*
- *What if she says "yes" just out of pity?*

The more he contemplates the many negative scenarios that could occur, the more he feels the pain of rejection. **He begins to convince himself that the risk is not worth it.** After all, there are *so many* possible negative scenarios and only one positive one in which she says "yes" and eventually becomes his girlfriend!

Is that really worth the potential pain of rejection and awkwardness?

What would you tell Raju to do?

According to a study, more than 70% of people would tell Raju to take the chance. Because what does it really matter if she says "no"? Plus, he will have taken the first step to getting over his fear of talking to women!

Sure, it may be a little bit awkward, but isn't living a life in fear worse? **He has to summon the courage to put himself out there sometime!**

But, when the tables are turned, and people are asked what they would do in the same situation, **only 30% of people said they would ask the girl out!** It seems that we have courage for others, but still fear the consequences for ourselves.

You have probably been in a similar position to Raju at some point in your life. It may not have been to ask a girl out for a coffee or movie, but *any* situation where we have to make ourselves vulnerable feels the same way.

- *Family Members in the Family Business & Taking Decision.*
- *Asking for New Orders or Referrals from Customers.*
- *Starting a new Business or Partnership.*
- *Venturing into Diversification.*
- *Asking for Money*
- *Firing the Lazy People and Giving Constructive Feedback.*
- *Doing something New & Out of the Box*

It doesn't matter what the act of vulnerability is, we imagine all of the possible negative outcomes and fear what might happen. **We usually keep to ourselves.** We don't take that risk because we feel like it just is not worth it.

So how do we become as brave as when we are giving advice? How can we fear the short-term consequences less and be able to see the incredible benefits of being more vulnerable? The answer is by following the 10-10-10 Rule.

How to Apply the 10-10-10 Rule:

Put yourself back in Raju's shoes. Let's say that he decides that he is going to call her and ask her for a cup of coffee or a movie.

How will he feel about the decision 10 minutes after?

Maybe a little embarrassed and worried about what their project will be like if she says "no". But he will probably still feel proud that he overcame his fear and did it. But if she says "yes", he will feel elated! He will be proud of the fact that he overcame his fear and excited about the fact that he has a date with a girl that he really likes!

How will he feel about the decision 10 months after?

He will either have completely forgotten about the dreaded phone call if she said "no", or there's a chance that he could have a girlfriend!

How will he feel about the decision 10 years after?

He will either have completely forgotten about the girl, or there's a small chance he will have met his soul mate.

From this perspective, are the risks still greater than the potential payoff?

We have a tendency to overvalue the moments that are right in front of us. From our current lens, we can't see that decisions like these mean very little to our long-term happiness. So, in moments like this, it helps to change our perspective to think about things from a longer timeline.

Conclusion:

Making the right decision can be tough. We envision all of the nightmare scenarios that could possibly go wrong. When we are thinking about whether or not to "put ourselves out there" we get a distorted view of the risks and potential benefits.

But, when we look at the situation from 10 minutes, 10 months and 10 years from now, we see how insignificant the downsides are and how potentially big the upsides are! So, the next time you're afraid to be vulnerable, go through the 10-10-10 exercise. You may just find it easier to summon the willpower you need!

Action Exercise:

(Please Practice the following or any other situation which you think are taking up a lot of your time due to indecision and procrastination and the fear of failure, rejection or being ridiculed.

- *Family Members in the Family Business & Taking Decision.*
- *Asking for New Orders or Referrals from Customers.*
- *Starting a new Business or Partnership.*
- *Venturing into Diversification.*
- *Asking for Money*
- *Firing the Lazy People and Giving Constructive Feedback.*
- *Doing something New & Out of the Box*
- *Or anything in Personal & Family Life that you have always feared of doing or taking it up.*

The next time you come face to face with a tough decision to put yourself in a vulnerable situation, go through this mental exercise 10-10-10.

--*-*-*

"THE SECRET OF GETTING AHEAD

IS GETTING STARTED"

MARK TWAIN

--*-*-*

Business Strategy No. 5
THE BCG MATRIX

Introduction:

The Boston Consulting group's product portfolio matrix (BCG) is designed to help with long-term strategic planning, to help a business consider growth opportunities by reviewing its portfolio of products to decide where to invest, to discontinue or develop products. It's also known as the Growth/Share Matrix.

The Matrix is divided into 4 quadrants derived on market growth and relative market share, as shown in the diagram.

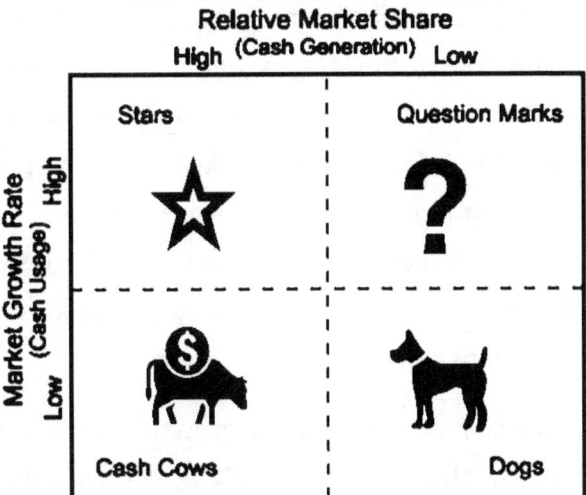

THE GROWTH SHARE MATRIX

1. **Dogs**: These are products with low growth or market share. The dogs are those product lines or business units that have a smaller market share in a mature and slow-growing industry. Usually, these product lines manage to earn what is put into

them, breaking-even and maintaining the market share. Generally, this unit is largely worthless to the company in terms of earning potential but may afford other benefits to the company such as the creation of jobs as well as synergies that assist other business units. These benefits may be enough for the company to keep this business unit active despite its less than exciting position.

2. **Question marks or Problem Child**: Products in high growth markets with low market share. The unknowns (also called question marks or problem children) are those business units that have a smaller market share in a high-growth market. This is where most businesses will start from and at this point the business unit has the potential to grow market share and turn into a star or lose further marker share and turn into dogs when the growth of the market itself declines. Careful study and analysis are required for business units in this category to assess their potential and worth. If any potential is seen then further investment can be made into them.

3. **Stars**: Products in high growth markets with high market share. As the name makes clear, stars are those business units that have a large market share in a fast-growing industry. These product lines have a clearly visible market or niche leading path and require large amounts of funding to ensure that they can fight of competitors and maintain their growth rate. Companies aim to turn stars into their next cash cows with the inevitable

decline in the growth of the industry. This can happen potentially if they are able to maintain their position as a market leader. If this does not happen, then stars can turn into dogs.

4. **Cash Cows**: Products in low growth markets with high market share. The product lines that fall within this category enjoy a large share of the market in a slow-growing industry. This means that they are able to generate revenues in greater amounts than the investment required to maintain their business. The product line may be considered boring and settled in a mature market, with the company holding it to continue to generate revenues. The company will attempt to milk these as much as possible with as little investment as possible.

How to use the BCG Matrix?

To look at each of these quadrants, here are some tips:

Dogs: The usual marketing advice is to remove any dogs from your product portfolio as they are a drain on resources. However, some can generate ongoing revenue with little cost. For example, in the automotive sector, when a car line ends, there is still a need for spare parts.

Question marks: Named this, as it's not known if they will become a star or drop into the dog quadrant. These products often require significant investment to push them into the star quadrant. The challenge is that a lot of investment may be required to get a return.

For example, Rovio, creators of the very successful Angry Birds game have developed many other games you may not have heard of. Computer games companies often develop hundreds of games before gaining one successful game. It's not always easy to spot the future star and this can result in potentially wasted funds.

Stars: Can be the market leader though require ongoing investment to sustain. They generate more ROI than other product categories.

Cash Cows: 'Milk these products as much as possible without killing the cow! Often mature, well established products. The company Procter & Gamble which manufactures Pampers nappies to Lynx deodorants has often been described as a 'cash cow company'.

Use the model as an overview of your products, rather than detailed analysis. **If market share is small, use the 'relevant market share' axis is based on your competitors rather than entire market.**

Benefits of the BCG Matrix:

- Easy to perform;
- Helps to understand the strategic positions of business portfolio;
- It's a good starting point for further more thorough analysis.

THE GROWTH SHARE MATRIX

Star	Problem child
High market growth	High market growth
High market share	Low market share
Cash neutral	Cash absorbing
Hold	Build
Cash cow	**Dog**
Low market growth	Low market growth
High market share	Low market share
Cash generating	Cash neutral
Harvest or milk	Divest

--*-*-*

"THE ONLY STRATEGY THAT IS
GUARANTEED TO FAIL IS NOT
TAKING RISK"

MARK ZUCKERBERG

--*-*-*

Business Strategy No. 6
EISENHOWER BOX - FIRST THINGS FIRST

Introduction:

Eisenhower was the 34th President of the United States, serving two terms from 1953 to 1961. Eisenhower had an incredible ability to sustain his productivity not just for weeks or months, but for decades. And for that reason, it is no surprise that his methods for time management, task management, and productivity have been studied by many people.

His most famous productivity strategy is known as the Eisenhower Box and it's a simple decision-making tool that you can use right now. Let's talk about how to be more productive and how Eisenhower's strategy works.

Eisenhower's strategy for taking action and organizing your tasks is simple. Using the decision matrix below, you will separate your actions based on four possibilities.

- Urgent and important (tasks you will do immediately).
- Important, but not urgent (tasks you will schedule to do later).
- Urgent, but not important (tasks you will delegate to someone else).
- Neither urgent nor important (tasks that you will eliminate).

The great thing about this matrix is that it can be used for broad productivity plans ("How should I spend my time each week?") and for smaller, daily plans ("What should I do today?"). Knowing what is **Important** rather than simply responding to what is **Urgent** is First Things first. Shifting the focus from Urgency to the Importance. **The Main thing is to keep the Main thing the Main thing**.

The Difference Between Urgent and Important

"What is important is seldom urgent and what is urgent is seldom important." - Dwight Eisenhower

Urgent means a task requires immediate attention like crisis, pressing problems, emails, phone calls. These are the to-do's that shout "Now!" Urgent tasks put us in a reactive mode, one marked by a defensive, negative, hurried, and narrowly-focused mindset.

Important means tasks that contribute to our long-term mission, values, and goals. When we focus on important activities we operate in a responsive mode, which helps us remain calm, rational, and open to new opportunities.

There are several methods, techniques, tools, planners, etc., to manage and control our time. In fact, we have experienced three generations of time Management. We've been told to work harder, learn to do things better & faster, use new devices such as files, organizers, planners, schedules etc. to be able to do well.

But these do not click. We get frustrated. We feel that something is wrong somewhere. Because working faster and harder do not yield the desired results.

Generations of Time Management

- 1st – Reminders, to do lists etc.
- 2nd – Planers, Appointment books
- 3rd – Prioritization

1st & 2nd generation of Time Management help as Memory Aids. The 3rd generation of Time Management can be compared to a Car Travel, using a wrong map. We have a better car, good road etc. It facilitates speedy travel, offers good mileage. But the **Wrong Map** will take us to the wrong place, faster!

If we keep doing what we've been doing, we're going to keep getting what we're getting. One definition of insanity is to keep doing the same thing and expect different results. We need to move beyond Time Management to Life Leadership – to a 4th generation based on paradigm that will create quality of life results.

4th generation of Time Management is based on **Importance Paradigm**. Free yourself from the '**Urgency addiction**'.

Life is hectic. What is important to me is being swept away in the current of what is important to everybody else. The enemy of best is 'good'. It is the question of choice – first things first – what contributes to your life.

The Eisenhower Decision Matrix

Business thinker **Stephen Covey** popularized the Eisenhower's Decision Principle in his book, **The 7 Habits of Highly Effective People**. In that book, Covey created a decision matrix to help individuals make the distinction between what's important and not important and what's urgent and not urgent. The matrix consists of a square divided into four boxes, or four quadrants.

Time Management Matrix (URGENT / IMPORTANT)

	URGENT	NOT URGENT
	Quadrant 1	**Quadrant 2**
IMPORTANT	• Crises • Pressing Problems • Deadline driven projects • Meetings • Preparation – Event, Function • Last Minute Rush • Emergency	• Vision, Mission, Goals • Clarifying Values & Principles • Strategy Development • Planning, Preparing, Preventing • Team & Relationship Building • Delegation • Learning & Upgrading
	Quadrant 3	**Quadrant 4**
NOT IMPORTANT	• Interruptions like some Phone Calls, Meetings, Visitors, Reports, Email etc. which are Not Important and you can do it later. • Many proximate, pressing matters, Popular activities where you cannot say "NO"	• Trivia Work like checking SPAM Email & SMS • Whatapps Messages • Watching Mindless TV • Water Cooler Chats, Gossips • Time Pass "Escape" activities • Illusion of Recreation

Conclusion:

It can be hard to eliminate time wasting activities if you aren't sure what you are working toward. There are two questions that can help clarify the entire process behind the Eisenhower Method.

Those two questions are...

- **What am I working toward?**
- **What are the core values that drive my life?**

Answering these questions will help you clarify the categories for certain tasks in my life. Deciding which tasks to do and which tasks to delete becomes much easier when you are clear about what is important to you.

The Eisenhower Method is useful decision-making tool for increasing your productivity and eliminating the behaviors that take up mental energy, waste time, and rarely move you toward my goals.

--*-*-*

"EVERYONE WANTS TO LIVE ON TOP
OF THE MOUNTAIN, BUT ALL THE
HAPPINESS AND GROWTH OCCURS
WHILE YOU'RE CLIMBING IT."

ANDY ROONEY

--*-*-*

Business Strategy No. 7
THE PARETOE PRINCIPLE (80-20 RULE)

Introduction:

The Pareto principle also known as the 80/20 rule states that, for many events, roughly 80% of the effects come from 20% of the causes. It is named after economist Vilfredo Pareto who originally referred to the observation that 80% of Italy's wealth belonged to only 20% of the population.

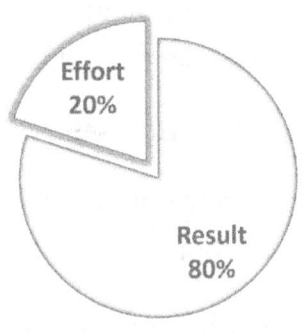

More generally, the Pareto Principle is the observation (not law) that most things in life are not distributed evenly. It can mean all of the following things:

- 20% of the efforts gives 80% of the result
- 20% of the sales generate 80% of the profit
- 20% of the input creates 80% of the result
- 20% of the workers produce 80% of the result
- 20% of the customers create 80% of the revenue
- 20% of the bugs cause 80% of the crashes
- 20% of the features cause 80% of the usage
- 20% of the fault causes 80% of the breakdown
- And on and on...

Understand that the numbers don't have to be "20%" and "80%" exactly. The key point is that **most things in life (effort, reward, output) are not distributed evenly – some contribute more than others**. The key point is that most things are **not** 1/1, where each unit of "input" (effort, time, labor) contributes exactly the same amount of output.

How is 80-20 Useful?

The Pareto Principle helps you realize that the majority of results come from a minority of inputs. Knowing this, if...

- 20% of workers contribute 80% of results: Focus on rewarding these employees.
- 20% of bugs contribute 80% of crashes: Focus on fixing these bugs first.
- 20% of customers contribute 80% of revenue: Focus on satisfying these customers.

The examples go on. The point is to realize that you can often focus your effort on the 20% that makes a difference, instead of the 80% that doesn't add much.

In economics terms, there is **diminishing marginal benefit**. This is related to the law of diminishing returns: each additional hour of effort, each extra worker is adding less "value" to the final result. By the end, you are spending lots of time on the minor details.

Examples of Application of Pareto's Principle

- **Marketing Investment:** The 80/20 rule has a few marketing-related applications. One application relates to how money is spent on advertising and other marketing campaigns. In general, 20 percent of marketing messages produce 80 percent of your campaign results. Understanding which of your investments produce the greatest results lets you eliminate some of the costs associated with less productive techniques. This improves your marketing efficiency and returns.

- **Product Mix:** From a product perspective, 80 percent of a typical company's revenue is derived from 20 percent of its products or services. These products are sometimes referred to as cash cows since they drive much of the business' results. You can utilize this awareness in a couple ways. You can emphasize the value of your core products in a better way to target customers. You can also expand your business by targeting new customer groups that have the most impact on products and services.

- **Profits:** One of the most useful applications of the 80/20 rule in marketing relates to profits. A typical business earns approximately 80 percent of its profits from the top 20 percent of its customer base. This knowledge enables companies to focus on maintaining relationships with these top customers. Loyalty and frequency programs are intended to offer the best value and experiences to customers who provide the best results.

- **Customer Pyramid:** The customer pyramid approach is a way to expand on the Pareto Principle and further break down your customer base for business efficiency. At the top of your pyramid is the platinum level, or the top 20 percent of customers. Just below are the gold customers. In a highly profitable company, gold customers also contribute to profits and might eventually become part of the core group. Getting them engaged in loyalty programs is helpful. The next tier, the silver group, may or may not include profit-generating customers. These are more cost-conscious customers, so the key to retaining them is to provide basic services at minimal costs. The bottom of your pyramid are the lead weight customers. These customers are typically unprofitable. They demand time, resources and services, but are unwilling to pay for them.

Now Apply this 80/20 Rule in your Business

If you are given a choice to select from 2 currency notes, a Rs.50/- note and a Rs.500/- note, which will you choose and why? Definitely, you would choose Rs.500/-, rather than Rs.50/- because Rs.500/- is 10 times Rs.50/- rupee note.

Similarly, in your Business are you aware which is Rs.500/- & Rs.50/- note Business, the 80 percent of your business comes from 20 percent of your customers. The 20% customers are your Rs.500/- notes. Start identifying them.

Take some time off and think about this for a moment... If you're really getting 80 percent of your business from 20 percent of your customers, then you're getting the remaining 20 percent of your business is coming from the 80 percent of your customers.

Why invest so much time, effort and energy trying to serve the 80 percent of your customers that are generating only 20 percent of your business?

With this in mind, let me ask you 3 questions:

- How much time is being spent servicing people that don't buy very much from you?
- How much time is spent answering questions from people who bought from you last year - and aren't a current customer?
- How many people call you, ask lots of questions, take up your time, and then buy from someone else?
- When you're wasting your precious time, effort, and resources dealing with these people, you aren't giving yourself the opportunity to find new prospects who could become valued and loyal customers. And you wonder why you're so tired and business is so slow.
- Take a look at how much time you are spending calling on, servicing, or answering questions from people who don't do business with you.

Stop wasting your time and start analyzing the 80/20 in your business.

Here are 3 things you can do that will help you eliminate people who keep you busy, waste your time, and never do business with you:

1. Keep track of everybody you speak daily.
2. Keep detailed notes of everything that was discussed, how much time they took up, how much they purchase, and how timely they are about paying their bills. (Customers who don't pay their bills are BAD customers.)
3. Schedule regular follow-up calls and meetings so you don't lose track and forget about your good customers.

Spend more time serving the 20 percent of your customers that generate 80 percent of your business and let someone else look after everybody else. Now you've more time to find, meet, and sell new customers that have the quality and characteristics of your best customers. You'll quickly begin to close more sales, make more money, and have more fun.

You'll enjoy collecting Rs.500/-, so friends it is high time you start identifying the Rs.500/- and be aware of it.

Business Strategy No. 8
RAY CARTER'S 10C MODEL

Introduction

Ray Carter's 10C Model is named after Ray Carter who originally devised 7 Cs of effective supplier evaluation. This has since been extended to 10 and they offer a very clear focus for anyone who is involved in either selecting or evaluating Suppliers or Contractors.

Why should I use the Carter's 10C?

- The Carter 10C model is an internationally recognized approach and taught in procurement studies.
- A standard selection framework for selecting suppliers.
- Selecting the right supplier includes much more than a focus purely on cost.
- Makes supplier selection where wide range of variables are to be considered easy, simple & time-saving.
- Standard criteria can help level the playing field whilst also giving you a standardized procedure removing some of the guesswork from the process. For example, you may have found a supplier that offered a good price, but later realized that its quality standards were low, or that its communication was unacceptably poor.
- Mismatches between your needs and a supplier's offerings can add costs, cause delays, and even damage your

organization's reputation – for example, if the equipment or resources supplied are substandard. The "10 Cs of Supplier Evaluation" help you avoid problems like these.

- The checklist helps you to set out your organization's needs, understand how suppliers can meet them, and identify the right supplier for you.
- You can use it to analyze different aspects of a supplier's business: examining all 10 elements of the checklist will give you a broad understanding of the supplier's effectiveness and ability to deliver.
- The checklist can also help you negotiate a lower price with a supplier.
- For business-critical resources, for situations where you will be spending a lot of money, or where you want a long-term relationship with a supplier, it's worth putting a lot of effort into supplier evaluation.

Let's look at how you can apply the 10 Cs to find the supplier that will best fit your organization's needs and values.

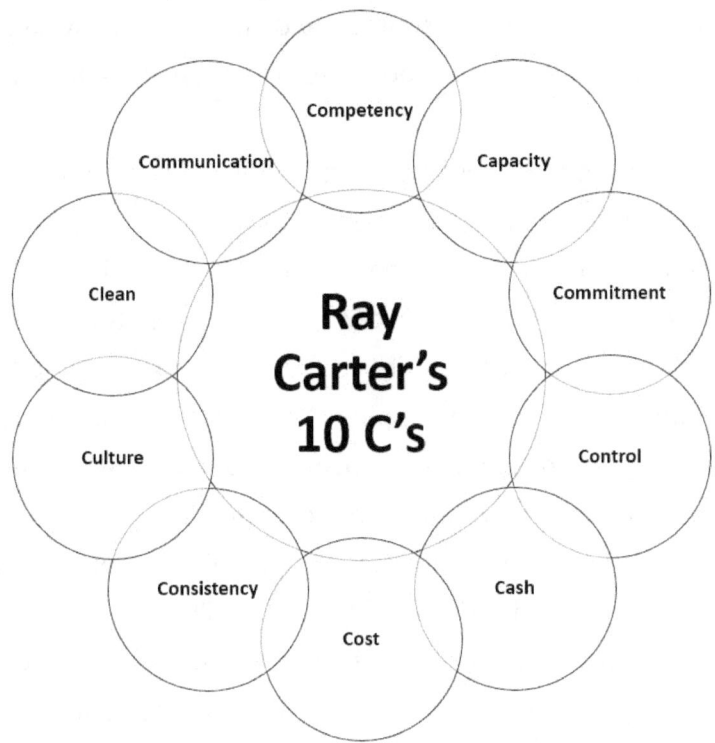

1. **Competency** – Does your supplier have the ability to deliver the products you require? Make a thorough assessment of the supplier's capabilities measured against your needs, but then also look at what other customers think. How happy are they with the supplier? Have they encountered any problems? And why have former customers changed supplier?

2. **Capacity** – Does the supplier have sufficient capacity to provide the products you require? Capacity can include equipment, human resources and materials. How quickly will it be able to respond to the market and supply fluctuations?

3. **Commitment** – Does your supplier have the commitment to maintain suitable quality performance? The supplier also needs to show that it is committed to you, for the duration of the time that you expect to work together. This is particularly important if you're planning a long-term relationship with the supplier. You'll need evidence of its ongoing commitment to delivering to your requirements, whatever the needs of its other customers.

4. **Control** – Is your supplier in control of their policies, procedures, and supply chain. How will it ensure that it delivers consistently and reliably, particularly if it relies on scarce resources, and particularly if these are controlled by another organization?

5. **Cash** – Does your supplier have a solid financial standing? Cash-positive firms are in a much better position to weather the ups and downs of an uncertain economy.

6. **Cost** – What is the cost of products from the supplier? How does this compare with the other firms that you're considering?

7. **Consistency** – Does the supplier guarantee a consistent product of the standard quality?

8. **Culture** – Does the supplier share the same cultural values as your organization? For example, what if your organization's most important value is quality, and your main supplier cares more about meeting deadlines? This mismatch could mean that it's willing to cut corners in a way that could prove to be unacceptable to you.

9. **Clean** – This refers to this supplier's commitment to sustainability, and its adherence to environmental laws and best practices. What is it doing to lighten its environmental footprint? Ask to see evidence of any green accolades or credentials that it's earned. Does this supplier treat its people well; and does it have a reputation for doing business ethically?

10. **Communication** – What tools will you utilize to communicate with your supplier? Who will be your contact person at this firm? It's also important to find out how the supplier will handle communications in the event of a crisis. How quickly will it notify you if there's a supply disruption? How will that communication take place? And will you be able to reach senior people, if you need to? Ex: Email, Office/Mobile Number etc.

These 10 Cs offer a very comprehensive means of ensuring that a rigorous approach is adopted with regard to supplier evaluation and that it is fair to all potential suppliers!

--*-*-*

"THE ONLY PLACE WHERE SUCCESS COMES BEFORE WORK IS IN THE DICTIONARY"

ALBERT EINSTEIN

--*-*-*

Business Strategy No. 9
TIM BAKER'S 4 STRATEGIES OF INFLUENCE

Introduction:

Tim Baker's Influencing Framework, describes four strategies of influence, viz: **Investigation, Calculation, Motivation, and Collaboration.** Each of these combines either a Push or a Pull style with either a Logical or an Emotional approach.

PUSH STYLE	PULL STYLE	www.ShabbarSuterwala.com
INVESTIGATION	**CALCULATION**	LOGICAL APPROACH
MOTIVATION	**COLLABORATION**	EMOTIONAL APPROACH

Tim Baker's 4 Strategies of Influence

A Push style is a direct, assertive way of getting your point across, while a Pull style is an indirect, subtle way of persuading others. And to influence Logically, you'll use facts and rational argument to make your case, while, with the Emotional approach, you "tug at people's heart strings" to get your way.

LOGICAL	EMOTIONAL
• Facts	• Feelings
• Evidence	• Perceptions
• Rational	• Values
• Structure	• Flexibility
• Measurement	• Morale

PUSH	PULL
• Driving	• Enabling
• Proposing	• Testing Understanding
• Giving Information	• Seeking Information
• Blocking / Shutting Out	• Building / Opening Up
• Taking the Idea to the Person	• Getting the Person to come to the Idea

Think about which characteristics you tend to favour most of the time when working with other people.

- **Driving – Enabling:** *Driving* means the influencer is attempting to take others on a path he or she has specifically clearly laid out. *Enabling* is more about the influencer facilitating a process so that others are persuaded to find their own path to a broad destination.

- **Proposing - Testing Understanding:** *Proposing* entail the influencer offering suggestions based on their own experience or vision. *Testing Understanding* on the other hand is evaluating an incident and facilitating course corrections in a collaborative fashion.

- **Giving information - Seeking information:** *Giving information* is informing an inspiring a group so they may be better equipped to undertake a task. *Seeking information* is testing the group's understanding of a task and adjusting an approach based on teamwork.

- **Blocking/Shutting out - Building/Opening up:** *Blocking and Shutting out* is based on asserting a position on an issue in a compelling way that effectively eliminates other possibilities. *Building and Opening up* is the reverse approach: it is about exploring a range of possibilities and then reaching agreement.

- **Taking the idea to the person - Getting the person to come to the idea:** When a leader decides to sell an idea to their team, this is a more direct style of influence characteristic of *taking the idea to the person*. Conversely, when the leader encourages the team to talk through an approach and get agreement on a way forward, they are adopting a pull style of influence characteristic of *getting the person to come to the idea*.

Which style do I use, Push or Pull?

The rationale for using the Push Style is that people are influenced by compelling proposals, well supported by factual argument or a clear and motivating vision of the future. This implies a more direct and systematic manner of influencing. While the rationale for using the Pull Style is that people are more influenced readily when their needs, motives, aspirations and concerns are uncovered and catered for.

Which styles is the one you use most of the time when you are trying to persuade someone else about something? One is not necessarily better than the other; each is effective in the right place, at the right time, with the right circumstances, and the right person.

Investigators:

- Draw on facts and figures to support a logical and methodical approach.
- Collect two main types of information i.e. Background Data, which informs their view of the world, and Task-Related Data, which is gathered for a specific purpose.
- Once they have the all information they need, then they weave it all into an appealing and convincing argument.
- Using tangible facts and hard data alongside more abstract, visionary ideas allows them to communicate more effectively.
- Example is Al Gore

Calculator:

- Tend to use logic to influence and are good debaters.
- They give time and effort to in-depth analysis and the creation of a well-structured argument.

- They have the ability to weigh options, the capacity to provide feedback like the positives of a proposal & highlight the weaknesses in the current position.
- Example: Margaret Thatcher

Motivator:

- They use emotion and the "big picture" to communicate compelling visions of the future.
- They add structure to enthusiasm and maximize the impact of any presentation you have to give
- They will gain the audience's attention, and leave members with specific actions that they can take afterward.
- They use their natural charisma and are more engaging, likeable and inspiring.
- They Concentrate on their body language, to help others to feel good, and show empathy, assertiveness and confidence.
- Example: Martin Luther-King

Collaborator:

- They use motivation, too, but they persuade people by involving them in the decision, thus engaging people's heart & mind.

- They build bonds and develop trust between team members. This helps people to own the process of change for themselves.
- They play the role of a facilitator rather than trying to convince team members logically.
- They share the power, have the capacity to listen actively and a willingness to communicate openly.
- Example: Mother Teresa
- The modern workplace is changing, and holding a senior position within an organization no longer automatically means that you can influence your team members. Flatter workforce structures mean that we often have to convince both bosses and colleagues of the merits of our strategy or idea. This means that we need a range of influencing tactics at our disposal, to ensure that we are comfortable influencing different people at different times and in different situations.

Further here are some practical techniques and methods to enhance each of these four influencing strategies:

Understand the Power Bases:

- **The Power of Position to Influence**
    - o   Legitimate Power (Position)
    - o   Coercive Power (Threat)
    - o   Reward Power (Favours)
- **Personal Power**

- o   Connection Power (Network)
- o   Expert Power (Skills)
- o   Information Power (Knowledge)
- o   Referent Power (Respect)

Nine Tools to Build Personal Power.

- Tool 1 – Who you know and what they know
- Tool 2 – Develop your knowledge and expertise
- Tool 3 – Building trust and rapport
- Tool 4 – Be logic and rational
- Tool 5 – Build alliances
- Tool 6 – Build rapport
- Tool 7 – Be a valued asset
- Tool 8 – Assertively persuade
- Tool 9 – Be upwardly appealing

For Leadership Development:

Investigation Tools

- Using third party endorsements
- Structured interviews
- Conduct a Survey
- Process Mapping
- 360 Degree Feedback

Calculation Tools

- Force-field analysis
- Cost-benefit analysis
- After action reviews

Motivation Tools

- Team values charter
- GROW model
- Storytelling
- Good news stories
- SWOT Analysis

Collaboration Tools

- Begin with the end in mind
- Giving effective feedback
- Using a problem-solving approach
- Paraphrasing & Active Listening
- Johari Window

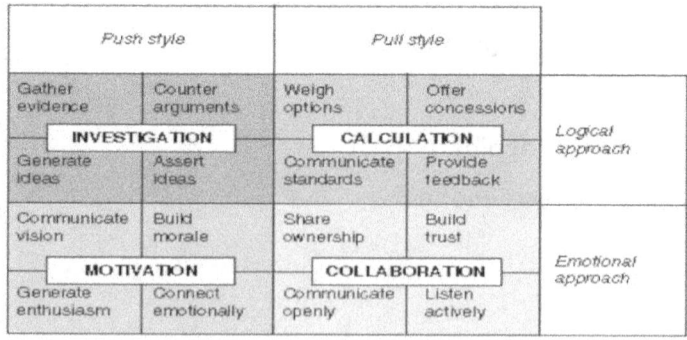

Push style		Pull style		
Gather evidence	Counter arguments	Weigh options	Offer concessions	Logical approach
INVESTIGATION		CALCULATION		
Generate ideas	Assert ideas	Communicate standards	Provide feedback	
Communicate vision	Build morale	Share ownership	Build trust	Emotional approach
MOTIVATION		COLLABORATION		
Generate enthusiasm	Connect emotionally	Communicate openly	Listen actively	

Business Strategy No. 10
THE TOYOTA 3M MODEL - MUDA, MURA, MURI

Introduction:

Toyota has developed its production system around eliminating three enemies Muda (Waste), Mura (Unevenness) and Muri (Overburden).

MUDA	MURA	MURI
(Waste)	(Unevenness)	(Overburden)

When people think of waste, they usually only think about all of the scrap material that gets thrown away, they often forget about all of the other actions that waste our time, our resources and our MONEY.

The three enemies of lean can be found in both production and office processes. I even dare to say that they can be found more in office processes than in production processes. One reason for this is that production processes are visible. Everybody who walks through a factory can see the inventory waiting to be worked on. In the office environment however, processes are often hidden inside our computers, in mailboxes and IT-systems.

Though it is the goal of lean to reduce all three enemies of Lean, it might not be possible to completely remove all of them.

In terms of Muda, unless your factory is placed next to your customer, there will always be some sort of transport necessary to get the product to your customer. We should focus on reducing the transport time and costs as much as we can, but 100% reduction is not realistic.

The same holds for Muri. There can always be a time where machines or people have to give that little extra effort or time to make sure the customer demand is fulfilled. There is nothing wrong with this when you can thereby get a huge order of extra products or win over a new client. The problem exists when you are expecting this from your machines or people all the time, up to a point where a machine will burn down or a colleague burns out.

Finally, even Mura cannot always be reduced with 100%. When you are producing different products, they are bound to require different materials, a different way of working or even different process times. This is even more so in project work, where every project is different, or in the financial world, where a financial report needs to be delivered at the end of each month.

Muda and Types of Wastes

Muda is any activity or process that does not add value; a physical waste of your time, resources and ultimately your money. These wastes were categorized by Taiichi Ohno within the Toyota production system, they are;

1. **Transport**: The movement of product between operations, and locations or having to move materials, parts, or finished goods into or out of storage or between processes.

2. **Inventory**: The work in progress (WIP), stocks of finished goods and excess raw materials that a company holds causing longer lead times, obsolescence, damaged goods, transportation and storage costs. Also, extra inventory hides problems such as production imbalances, late deliveries from suppliers, defects, equipment downtime.

3. **Motion**: Any Unnecessary movement of an employees have to perform during the course of their work other than adding value to the part, such as reaching for, looking for, or stacking parts, tools, etc. Also, walking is waste.

4. **Waiting**: The Workers merely serving as watch persons for an automated machine, or having to stand around waiting for the next processing step, tool, supply, part, etc., or just plain having no work because of no stock, lot processing delays, equipment downtime, and capacity bottlenecks.

5. **Overproduction**: Producing items earlier or in greater quantities than needed by the customer. Producing earlier or more than is needed generates other wastes, such as over-staffing, storage and transportation costs because of excess inventory. Inventory can be physical inventory or a queue of information.

6. **Over-processing**: Taking unneeded steps to process the parts. Inefficiently processing due to poor tool and product design, causing unnecessary motion and producing defects. Waste is generated when providing higher quality products than is necessary. At times extra "work" is done to fill excess time rather than spend it waiting. Conducting operations/processes beyond those that customer requires.

7. **Defects**: Production of defective parts or correction. Repairing of rework, scrap, replacement production, and inspection means wasteful handling, time, and effort.

8. **Unused Employee Talent / Creativity**: Losing time, ideas, skills, improvements and learning opportunities by not engaging or listening to your employees. Or Failing to use the Talent and knowledge of all of your employees

9. **Resources**: failing to turn off lights and unused machines

10. **By-Products**: not making use of by-products of your process

Many "lean" initiatives fail to see past the elimination of Muda and believe that the point of Lean is to just eliminate waste. This leads to implementations that initially appear to save money but quickly fall apart and revert as problems such as customer demand fluctuations and supplier problems occur. They have failed to tackle the other forms of waste identified by Toyota;

Mura the Waste of Unevenness

Mura is the waste of unevenness or inconsistency, but what does this mean and how does it affect us?

Mura creates many of the types of wastes that we observe, Mura drives Muda! By failing to smooth our demand we put unfair demands on our processes and people and cause the creation of inventory and other wastes.

One obvious example is production processes where the manager is measured on monthly output, the department rushes like mad in the final week of the month to meet targets, using up components and producing parts not actually required. The first week of the month is then slow due to component shortages and no focus on meeting targets.

Muri the waste of Overburden

Muri is to cause overburden, by this we mean to give unnecessary stress to our employees and our processes. This is caused by Mura and a host of other failures in our system such as lack of training, unclear or no defined ways of working, the wrong tools, and ill thought out measures of performance.

Again, Mura causes Muda, the types of wastes are symptoms of our failure to tackle Mura and Muri within our processes not the root cause!

Remove Muda, Mura and Muri from your Organization

Lean Manufacturing is about the removal of waste; but not just Muda (non-value adding steps), it is about removing Mura and Muri too. In fact, by concentrating on solving Mura and Muri you prevent the creation of Muda.

You should first concentrate on ensuring that your Mura is removed and creating a level predictable flow; this in turn highlights the Muri (unreasonableness) within your system which can then be eliminated. By following this route, you will often eliminate the vast majority of Muda that is present within your system.

Muda, Mura and Muri can be eliminated or significantly reduced if you implement the various lean tools and principles. But don't just rush in to try and highlight and remove the Muda in the hope of making a quick impression, it will be a short-lived success as without tackling Mura and Muri you will find the other wastes of Muda returning to haunt you.

How to Eliminate Muda, Mura and Muri:

To Eliminate Muda, find the Root-Cause by asking 5W & 1H Questions:

Who	What	Where
Who does it? Who is doing it? Who should be doing it? Who else can do it? Who else should do it?	What to do? What is being done? What should be done? What else can be done? What else should be done?	Where to do it? Where is it done? Where should it be done? Where else can it be done? Where else should it be done?
When	**Why**	**How**
When to do it? When is it done? When should it be done? What other time can it be done? What other time should it be done?	Why does he do it? Why do it? Why do it there? Why do it then? Why do it that way?	How to do it? How is it done? How should it be done? Can this method be used in other areas? Is there any other way to do it?

To Eliminate Mura, Brainstorm the following Questions:

- Does it Happens Sometimes?
- Does it Happens at some places?
- Does it Happens to some people?

To Eliminate Muri, Ask the following Questions:

- Bend to work?
- Push Hard?
- Lift Weight?
- Repeat tiring Action?
- Wasteful Walk?
- Is Overburdening People resulting is safety & quality problems?
- Is Overburdening Equipment causing breakdowns & defects?

Business Strategy No. 11
THE 7 P's MARKETING MIX

Introduction:

Marketing is a continually evolving discipline and as such can be one that companies find themselves left very much behind the competition if they stand still for too long. One example of this evolution has been the fundamental changes to the basic Marketing mix. Where once there were 4 P's to explain the mix, nowadays it is more commonly accepted that a more developed 7 P's adds a much-needed additional layer of depth to the Marketing Mix with some theorists going even going further.

The Marketing Mix

Simply put the Marketing Mix is a tool used by Businesses and Marketers to help determine a product or brands offering. It is about putting the right product or a combination thereof in the place, at the right time, and

at the right price. The 4 P's have been associated with the Marketing Mix since their creation by E. Jerome McCarthy in 1960.

1. **Product:** Product refers to what you are selling, including all of the features, advantages and benefits that your customers can enjoy from buying your goods or services. When marketing your product, you need to think about the key features and benefits your customers want or need, including styling, quality, repairs, and accessories.

2. **Price:** This refers to your pricing strategy for your products and services and how it will affect your customers. You should identify how much your customers are prepared to pay, how much mark-up you need to cater for overheads, your profit margins and payment methods, and other costs. To attract customers and retain your competitive advantage, you may also wish to consider the possibility of discounts and seasonal pricing.

3. **Promotion:** These are the promotional activities you use to make your customers aware of your products and services, including advertising, sales tactics, promotions and direct marketing. Generally, these are referred to as marketing tactics.

4. **Place:** Place is where your products and services are seen, made, sold or distributed. Access for customers to

your products is key and it is important to ensure that customers can find you. If you are not a retail business, place is still an important part of your marketing. Your customers may need a quick delivery turnaround, or want to buy locally manufactured products.

In the late 70's it was widely acknowledged by Marketers that the Marketing Mix should be updated. This led to the creation of the Extended Marketing Mix in 1981 by Booms & Bitner which added 3 new elements to the 4 P's Principle. This now allowed the extended Marketing Mix to include products that are services and not just physical things.

5. **People:** People refer to the staff and salespeople who work for your business, including yourself. When you provide excellent customer service, you create a positive experience for your customers, and in doing so market your brand to them. In turn, existing customers may spread the word about your excellent service and you can win referrals.

6. **Process:** Process refers to the processes involved in delivering your products and services to the customer. It is also about being 'easy to do business with. Having good process in place ensures that you repeatedly deliver the same standard of service to your customers thus save time and money by increasing efficiency.

7. **Physical Evidence:** Physical evidence refers to everything your customers see when interacting with your business. Physical evidence pertains also to how a business and its products are perceived in the marketplace.

Marketing Mix is a basic concept, but if you don't understand it in detail or at all, then there is a fairly certain chance that you are missing out on the key ingredients that will ensure scalable success from the ground up.

It has been said many times in business that if you don't know your target market well enough and figured out what they exactly want, you'll commit entrepreneurial suicide and the business will inevitably fail.

On the other hand, you can be sure to attract mountains of profits when you have a deep understanding of these concepts. Understand this fully and you will know exactly how to maximize profits on your own sustainable business.

How to use the 7P's Marketing Mix in your Business:

1. Products:

A product has a certain life cycle that includes the growth phase, the maturity phase, and the sales decline phase. It is important for marketers to reinvent their products to stimulate more demand once it reaches the sales decline phase.

Marketers must expand the current product mix by diversifying and increasing the depth of your product line.

All in all, marketers must ask themselves the following question:

- What can I do to offer a better product to this group of people than my competitors?
- What does the client want from the service or product?
- How will the customer use it?
- Where will the client use it?
- What features must the product have to meet the client's needs?
- Are there any necessary features that you missed out?
- Are you creating features that are not needed by the client?
- What's the name of the product? Does it have a catchy name?
- What are the various combinations of sizes or colors available?

- How is the product different from the products of your competitors?
- What does the product look like?

2. Price:

Pricing always help shape the perception of your product in consumers eyes. Always remember that a low price usually means an inferior good in the consumers eyes as they compare your good to a competitor.

Consequently, prices too high will make the costs outweigh the benefits in customers eyes, and they will therefore value their money over your product. Be sure to examine competitors pricing and price accordingly.

When setting the product price, marketers should consider the perceived value that the product offers. There are three major pricing strategies, and these are:

- Market penetration pricing
- Market skimming pricing
- Neutral pricing

Some of the important questions that you should ask yourself when you are setting the product price:

- How much did it cost you to produce the product?
- What are the customers' perceived product value?

- Do you think that the slight price decrease could significantly increase your market share?
- Can the current price of the product keep up with the price of the product's competitors?

3. Promotion

Advertising typically covers communication methods that are paid for like television advertisements, radio commercials, print media, and internet advertisements. In contemporary times, there seems to be a shift in focus offline to the online world.

Public relations, on the other hand, are communications that are typically not paid for. This includes press releases, exhibitions, sponsorship deals, seminars, conferences, and events.

Word of mouth is also a type of product promotion. Word of mouth is an informal communication about the benefits of the product by satisfied customers and ordinary individuals. The sales staff plays a very important role in public relations and word of mouth.

It is important to not take this literally. Word of mouth can also circulate on the internet. Harnessed effectively and it has the potential to be one of the most valuable assets you have in boosting your profits online. An extremely good example of this is online social media and managing a firm's online social media presence.

In creating an effective product promotion strategy, you need to answer the following questions:

- How can you send marketing messages to your potential buyers?
- When is the best time to promote your product?
- Will you reach your potential audience and buyers through television ads?
- Is it best to use the social media in promoting the product?
- What is the promotion strategy of your competitors?

4. Place

You have to position and distribute the product in a place that is accessible to potential buyers. There are many distribution strategies, including:

- Intensive distribution
- Exclusive distribution
- Selective distribution
- Franchising

Here are some of the questions that you should answer in developing your distribution strategy:

- Where do your clients look for your service or product?

- What kind of stores do potential clients go to? Do they shop in a mall, in a regular brick and mortar store, in the supermarket, or online?
- How do you access the different distribution channels?
- How is your distribution strategy different from your competitors?
- Do you need a strong sales force?
- Do you need to attend trade fairs?
- Do you need to sell in an online store?

5. People

When a business finds people who genuinely believe in the products or services that the particular business creates, it's is highly likely that the employees will perform the best they can.

Give your business a competitive advantage by recruiting the right people, training them to develop their skills, and retaining good people.

Additionally, they'll be more open to honest feedback about the business and input their own thoughts and passions which can scale and grow the business.

This is a secret, "internal" competitive advantage a business can have over other competitors which can inherently affect a business's position in the marketplace.

6. Process

Make sure that you have a well-tailored process in place to minimize costs.

It could be your entire sales funnel, a pay system, distribution system and other systematic procedures and steps to ensure a working business that is running effectively.

Tweaking and enhancements can come later to "tighten up" a business to minimize costs and maximize profits.

7. Physical Evidence

The physical environment where you provide the product or service, the layout or interior design, your packaging, your branding. Physical evidence can also refer to your staff and how they dress and act.

Consider how your store's layout, fixtures and signage can build your brand and increase your sales.

A concept of this is branding. For example, when you think of "fast food", you think of McDonalds & KFC. When you think of "home appliances" Braun, Godrej & Bajaj. When you think of "two wheelers" Activa, Hero.

You immediately know exactly what their presence is in the marketplace, as they are generally market leaders and have established a physical evidence as well as psychological evidence in their marketing.

They have manipulated their consumer perception so well to the point where their brands appear first in line when an individual is asked to broadly "name a brand" in their niche or industry.

Is there an 8th P?

In some spheres of thinking, there are 8 P's in the Marketing Mix. The final P is Productivity and Quality. This came from the old Services Marketing Mix and is folded in to the Extended Marketing Mix by some marketers so what does it mean?

The 8th P of the Marketing Mix: Productivity & Quality - This P asks "is what you're offering your customer a good deal?" This is less about you as a business improving your own productivity for cost management, and more about how your company passes this onto its customers.

Conclusion:

Even after so many years the Marketing Mix is still very much applicable to a marketer's day to day work. A good marketer will learn to adapt the theory to fit with not only modern times but their individual business model.

By understanding the basic concept of the marketing mix and its extensions, you will be sure to achieve financial success whether it is your own business or whether you are assisting in your workplace's business success.

The ultimate goal of business is to make profits and this is a surefire, proven way to achieve this goal.

Product	Promotion	Price	Place	People	Process	Physical Evidence
• Quality	• Marketing Communication	• Positioning	• Trade Channels	• Individuals on Marketing Activities	• Customer Focus	• Sales / Staff Contact Experience of the Brand
• Image	• Personal Promotion	• List	• Sales Support	• Individuals on Customer Contact	• Business Led	• Product Packaging
• Branding	• Sales Promotion	• Discounts	• Channel Number	• Recruitment	• IT-Supported	• Online Experience
• Features	• PR	• Credit	• Segmented Channels	• Culture or Image	• Design Features	
• Variants	• Branding	• Payment Methods		• Training	• Research & Development	
• Mix	• Direct Marketing	• Free or Value Added Elements		• Skills		
• Support				• Remuneration		
• Customer Service						
• Use Occasion						
• Availability						
• Warranties						

Business Strategy No. 12
PORTER'S FIVE FORCES MODEL

Introduction:

One of the biggest threats to a business – startup or established, big or small is competition. Who is your competition? How are their actions in the marketplace going to affect your current bottom line and future planning?

To answer those questions, you must analyze the competition. One way to do that is by using Porter's Five Forces model to break them down into five distinct categories, designed to reveal insights.

Developed by Harvard Business School's Michael E. Porter in 1979, the five forces model looks at five specific factors that help determine whether or not a business can be profitable, based on other businesses in the industry, and how they can help you to analyze the strengths and weaknesses of your position.

According to Porter, the origin of profitability is identical regardless of industry. In that light, industry structure is what ultimately drives competition and profitability; not whether an industry produces a product or service, is emerging or mature, high-tech or low-tech, regulated or unregulated.

"If the forces are intense, as they are in such industries as airlines, textiles, and hotels, almost no company earns attractive returns on investment," Porter wrote. "If the forces are benign, as they are in industries such as software, soft drinks, and toiletries, many companies are profitable."

Understanding the Five Forces

Porter regarded understanding both the competitive forces and the overall industry structure as crucial for effective strategic decision-making. In Porter's model, the five forces that shape industry competition are:

1. Competitive Rivalry

This force examines how intense the competition currently is in the marketplace, which is determined by the number of existing competitors and what each is capable of doing. Rivalry competition is high when there are just a few businesses equally selling a product or service, when the industry is growing and when consumers can easily switch to a competitor's offering for little cost. When rivalry competition is high, advertising and price wars can ensue, which can hurt a business's bottom line.

Example: A shoe brand like Puma will face intense competition from Nike, Adidas and newer players. Nike and Adidas, which have considerably larger resources at their disposal, are making a play within the performance apparel market to gain market share in this up-and-coming product category. If the organization does not hold any fabric or process patents its product portfolio could be copied in the future.

2. Bargaining Power of Suppliers

This force analyzes how much power a business's supplier has and how much control it has over the potential to raise its prices, which, in turn, would lower a business's profitability. In addition, it looks at the number of suppliers available: The fewer there are, the more power they have. Businesses are in a better position when there are a multitude of suppliers.

Example: A diverse supplier base limits bargaining power. Foot ware products are produced by dozens of manufacturers located across multiple countries.

3. Bargaining Power of Customers

This force looks at the power of the consumer to affect pricing and quality. Consumers have power when there aren't many of them, but lots of sellers, as well as when it is easy to switch from one business's products or services to another. Buying power is low when consumers purchase products in small amounts and the seller's product is very different from any of its competitors.

Example: Puma customers include both wholesale customers as well as end customers. Wholesale customers Goods and the Sports Authority, hold a certain degree of bargaining leverage, as they could substitute Puma's products with those of competitors to gain higher margins. Bargaining power of end customers is lower as Puma enjoys strong brand recognition.

4. Threat of New Entrants

This force examines how easy or difficult it is for competitors to join the marketplace in the industry being examined. The easier it is for a competitor to join the marketplace, the greater the risk of a business's market share being depleted. Barriers to entry include absolute cost advantages, access to inputs, economies of scale and well-recognized brands.

Example: Large capital costs are required for branding, advertising and creating product demand, and hence limits the entry of newer players in the sports market. However, existing companies like Bata, Flexo in the sports shoes industry could enter the performance shoe market in the future.

5. Threat of substitute products or services

This force studies how easy it is for consumers to switch from a business's product or service to that of a competitor. It looks at how many competitors there are, how their prices and quality compare to the business being examined and how much of a profit those competitors are earning, which would determine if they can lower their costs even more. The threat of substitutes are informed by switching costs, both immediate and long-term, as well as a buyer's inclination to change.

Example: The demand for performance apparel, sports footwear and accessories is expected to continue, and hence we think this force does not threaten Puma in the foreseeable future.

Another Example of Porter's Five Forces Model of Cadbury

1. Competitive Rivalry

- Many businesses are competing against Cadbury and planning to take over the supremacy the company has for several years.

- Companies such as Nestle, Hershey's, Ferrero etc. are Cadbury's main rivals.
- Rivalry will always be strong among these companies because they sell from the same types of stores and their products are similar in some respects.

2. Bargaining Power of Suppliers
- Large number of suppliers.
- Cadbury has higher bargaining power than its suppliers.
- Cadbury can buy their raw materials for cheaper and more in bulk than a medium sized business could.

3. Bargaining Power of Customers
- Cadbury's customers are scattered all around the world and they are in billions.
- The increasing number of competitors that offers the same type of products at a lower cost might be the cause of customer loyalty alteration.
- No switching cost for customers

4. Threat of New Entrants
- The entry of competitors will be difficult because there are already well-established companies within this market.

- These include Mars, Nestle, Ferrero, Kraft, Hershey's and Lindt.
- This makes the barrier for entry very hard for another new company to start.
- They need high initial capital requirements.

5. **Threat of substitute products or services**
   - Supermarkets tend to copycat popular chocolates (for example Nestle Kit Kat) and provide their own brand on the shelves at a cheaper price.
   - Confectionary is brought for snacks and gifts. In this way, large no. of substitutes exists, like chips, fruits, beverages, etc.
   - Still chocolates scores higher than the substitutes as they are easy to preserve.

Conclusion:

- Cadbury is a well-established firm with customers spread in whole world.
- It is difficult for other firms to overcome its popularity.
- Economical distribution using proper supply chain management is necessity.
- Brand loyalty should be maintained.

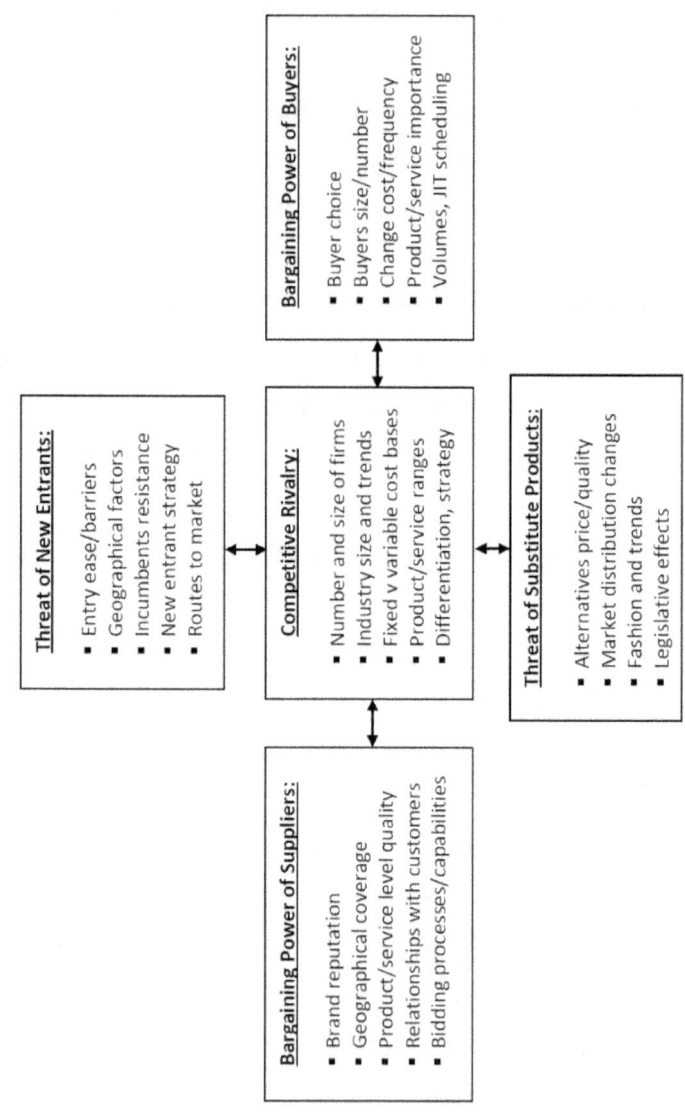

Threat of New Entrants:

- Entry ease/barriers
- Geographical factors
- Incumbents resistance
- New entrant strategy
- Routes to market

Competitive Rivalry:

- Number and size of firms
- Industry size and trends
- Fixed v variable cost bases
- Product/service ranges
- Differentiation, strategy

Bargaining Power of Buyers:

- Buyer choice
- Buyers size/number
- Change cost/frequency
- Product/service importance
- Volumes, JIT scheduling

Threat of Substitute Products:

- Alternatives price/quality
- Market distribution changes
- Fashion and trends
- Legislative effects

Bargaining Power of Suppliers:

- Brand reputation
- Geographical coverage
- Product/service level quality
- Relationships with customers
- Bidding processes/capabilities

Business Strategy No. 13
BOWMAN'S STRATEGY CLOCK

Introduction:

Bowman's Strategy Clock is a diagrammatic representation of the strategic options a business has to move in the customer value map – the relationship between the price a customer is willing to pay and the perceived customer value available from the product or service.

Many business owners and managers fall into the trap of thinking that they can just roll out a great product or service and instantly have a successful business.

While it helps to have something great to sell, you also need an overall strategy for your business to ensure that you are able to execute all parts of the operation efficiently. If you fail to create a good strategy, there is a chance that your business will fall short despite your best efforts. Bowman's Strategy Clock is one tool that you can use to find your place in the market.

Bowman's Strategy Cock is a method of strategy thinking that breaks down your potential strategy options into eight segments.

Most businesses should be able to find the right strategy for their operation within one of these eight options. All eight are illustrated below, along with a short description.

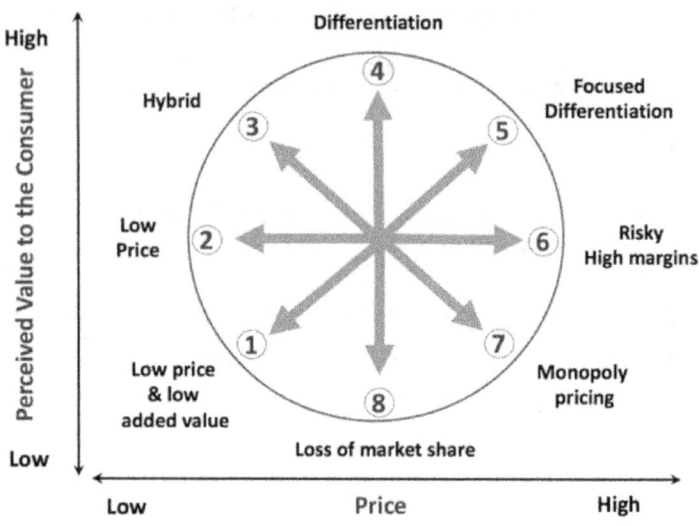

High

Perceived Value to the Consumer

Low

Low   Price   High

Differentiation

Hybrid

Focused
Differentiation

Low
Price

Risky
High margins

Low price
& low
added value

Monopoly
pricing

Loss of market share

1. Low Price - Low Added Value

This is the 'cheap' end of the market. Goods do not cost very much in this segment of the market, and they aren't of a very high quality, either. Most likely, you aren't going to select this part of the strategy clock as your ideal starting point for a business.

Instead, you might find that you have to try to compete at this level because you don't have another option. If the product or products that you are selling don't stand out from the rest of the market in any way, this is where you will be forced to fight for sales.

2. Low Price

When a company wants to sell a high volume of a product for a low margin, this is the area of the market where they choose to compete. Low cost leaders are often some of the biggest names in a particular market.

This is because it requires tremendous volume to turn a profit when selling your goods for a very low price. Smaller and medium sized businesses are unable to take this approach because the volumes they achieve simply will not sustain the business over the long term without a high retail price.

3. Hybrid

It isn't necessarily easy to slot yourself into the 'hybrid' segment of the market, but it can be a good place to land if you are able to do so successfully. When a company takes a hybrid approach, it means that: They are competing both on the quality of their products as well as the price.

If you can manage to build a reputation for selling quality goods while also being among the low-cost leaders in the segment, you will have a chance to grow customer loyalty and gain market share.

4. Differentiation

This part of the market is all about standing out from the crowd despite selling something that plenty of other businesses have to offer. The key to being differentiated in your market is branding.

You have to make an impression with your target audience, to the point that they will choose your product over other options even if you are selling at a higher price.

5. Focused Differentiation

The luxury brands that exist throughout many markets are said to use a focused differentiation strategy. The high price that these items sell for comes along with a higher perceived value in the minds of the consumers.

Margins are extremely high in this part of the market, but volume tends to be rather low. If you attempt to position your business in this market segment, you are going to need a strong marketing team to give your brand the image and recognition that it needs to move product at such a high price point.

6. Risky High Margins (Increased Price – Standard Product)

Most businesses will find this to be perhaps the most difficult position on the wheel to occupy. With this strategy, you are simply going to raise prices without changing anything about the quality of your product. Obviously risky, you could find a payoff in the form of larger profit margins – or you could find your sales numbers quickly slipping while you rush to lower prices once again.

This might be effective as a short-term strategy if your company is enjoying positive feedback from customers currently, but raising prices is a sure way to force the market to look elsewhere in the long term.

7. Monopoly Pricing (High Price – Low Value)

This strategy is really only an option for those who have a monopoly in their market. If you have entered a market niche that is light on competition, you may be able to charge high prices while offering a relatively low-quality product.

Of course, in the long run, other competitors are sure to enter the market at a lower price and you will be forced to adjust. Monopolies are very rare in today's global economy, and when they do arise, they never last for long before the competition arrives.

8. Loss of Market Share (Low Value – Standard Price)

The final strategy on the wheel is a losing one. If you are going to provide the market with a poor-quality product, yet you are going to try to sell it for the same price at higher quality products, you are going to lose in the end.

Many businesses have tried to 'cheat' this law of business by sneaking into the market with a poor product, but they never last long and they almost always lose money in the process.

Overview

Looking at the Strategy Clock in overview, you should be able to see that three of the positions (6, 7 and 8) are uncompetitive. These are the ones where price is greater than perceived value. Provided that the market is operating competitively, there will always be competitors that offer a higher perceived value for the same price, or the same perceived value for a lower price.

How to Use Bowman's Strategy Clock

Using Bowman's Strategy Clock is a great way to get an idea of how various businesses are competing in the market, and where you can fit into that market to carve out revenue for yourself.

Once you decide how it is that your competitors are trying to succeed in the market, you can look for opportunities and make your move.

Bowman's Strategy Clock is used to analyze the competitive position of a company's offerings in comparison to those of its competitors.

Key 8 Positions on the Clock Revisited:

1. **Low Price and Low Value Added**: The product is not differentiated and the customer perceives very little value, despite a low price.
2. **Low Price**: Businesses positioning themselves here look to be the low-cost leaders in a market. Margins on each product are low, but the high volume of output can still generate high overall profits.
3. **Hybrid**: This involves an element of low price and some product differentiation. It can be a very effective strategy if the added value is offered consistently.
4. **Differentiation**: This requires high quality product with strong brand awareness and loyalty.
5. **Focused Differentiation**: This the strategy adopted by luxury brands, which aim to achieve premium prices by highly targeted segmentation, promotion and distribution.
6. **Increased Price-Standard Product**: This is a very short-term strategy as the opportunity to sell for a high price without justification seldom lasts long.
7. **High Price-Low Value**: This is only sustainable where the organization has a monopoly.
8. **Low Value-Standard Price**: Setting a standard price for a product with low perceived value is likely to lead to an ongoing loss of market share.

--*-*-*

"THE VALUE OF AN IDEA LIES IN THE USING OF IT."

THOMAS EDISON

--*-*-*

Business Strategy No. 14

LAFLEY & MARTIN'S 5 STEP STRATEGY MODEL

Introduction:

P&G's Ex-CEO used this 5-Step formula to make Billion Dollar decisions. If you would like to develop a winning strategy for your own business, consider using Lafley and Martin's Five-Step Strategy Model. This is a relatively new model which was published in a 2013 book, making it one of the most-modern strategy models in business.

Answering those questions requires deep knowledge of your business and market, and you have to make sure they're integrated, but the framework is extremely easy.

Where most people think that they need to have the best product or service in the world in order to win, success in business is actually as much about strategy as it is about the actual product that is being sold. Of course, it helps to have a great product, but you need an excellent strategy to match.

People just avoid strategy because they hate making real choices. But to succeed in business – no matter what business you are in – you are going to need a great strategy.

By working through the five steps that are included in this model, you should emerge with a clear concept of how your business is going to be run from this day forward.

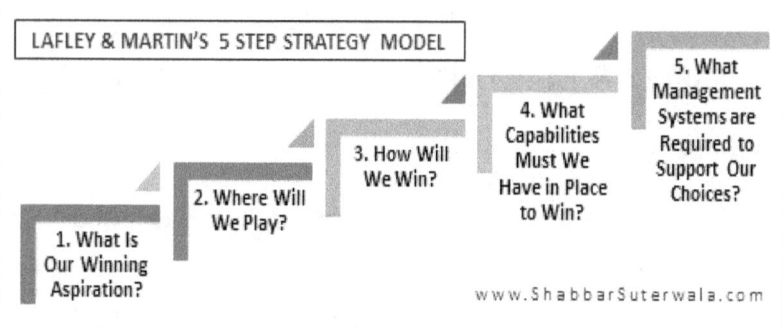

LAFLEY & MARTIN'S 5 STEP STRATEGY MODEL

5. What Management Systems are Required to Support Our Choices?

4. What Capabilities Must We Have in Place to Win?

3. How Will We Win?

2. Where Will We Play?

1. What Is Our Winning Aspiration?

www.ShabbarSuterwala.com

1) What Is Our Winning Aspiration?

Quite simply, this is the goal of the organization. Of course, it should be a bit more specific than just stating that you would like to 'make money'. All for-profit businesses want to make money, so that doesn't really help you get anywhere. What it is that you are going to do in order to make that money? Are you trying to dominate a specific market, or are you just looking for a piece of a big market? It is important to be specific even at this top level, as your answers to this question will influence decisions you make later on.

The best way to think about this question is to picture what success would look like in the future. If your organization is being successful five years from now, what would that look like? You should be optimistic, but realistic at the same time. For instance, if you sell some form of technology, you likely aren't going to topple the major players in the tech game, but that doesn't mean you can't hit your own marks for success.

2) Where Will We Play?

Once you know what it will look like to win, you then need to decide exactly where you are going to 'play' in order to achieve that victory. This question demands that you identify both the markets and the customers that you are going to pursue. For some businesses, such as those that sell directly to consumers, the answers to this question will be easy.

For example, if you produce a small product that is easy to ship, and you are selling direct to consumers, you will likely set up a website in addition to selling on other established e-commerce sites. However, for businesses that are going to sell to distributors or other intermediaries, identifying specific markets may take a bit more time and effort.

3) How Will We Win?

Now that you know where you are going to be competing in the market, the next step to deal with is the strategy that you are going to use to make sure you come out on top. You are going to face competition in whatever slice of the market you have decided to enter, so you will need to think long and hard about how you can position your product or service to stand out from the rest. If you take this step for granted, you will likely find that your competition remains a step ahead for years to come.

You don't necessarily have to have a complex strategy in place at this level to come out on top, but it does need to be a good strategy that has a real chance to succeed.

You could plan on winning the market based on lower cost, higher quality, faster turnaround times, or some combination of those three. Business is very simple when you boil it down to the basic level – consumers want good products and services for fair prices. Focus on those tenets and you will be headed in the right direction.

4) What Capabilities Must We Have in Place to Win?

This is the infrastructure that supports the plans you have developed. In order to enter the selected markets, and win in those markets, you will need a specific set of capabilities in place within your organization. What are you going to need to do in order to meet your goals at higher strategy levels?

For instance, if you have decided that you are going to win through offering lower prices, what capabilities to do you need in order to be able to sell your goods at a low price point? Without the capabilities necessary to meet your higher-level goals, the organization is destined to fail.

5) What Management Systems Are Required to Support Our Choices?

All organizations are driven forward by people, even if there is plenty of technology in place within the company as well. Without good people working toward a common goal, everything else that you have done to this point will be wasted.

This final step of the strategy process demands that you take the time and effort to build management teams which will be able to support the organizational goals and strategies that have been put into place.

Conclusion:

There is a lot to learn from using this model within your own organization, as it can help you to quickly create a top-down set of strategies that will keep your business moving in the proper direction for months and (hopefully) years to come.

Businesses without specifically-outlined strategies tend to 'float around' until they are eventually knocked out by superior competition. Don't let that happen to you. Use this five-step process to clearly define all of your strategies and look forward to a long and prosperous future.

All of the above questions played a role in the decision to divest; these were areas in **which P&G could win, Lafley said**. "They were demographically more attractive, they were structurally more attractive, lower capital, higher margin, and frankly they were better fit with our core competencies, deep understanding of consumers, the creation of known brands, and innovation, they were just a better fit with where we wanted to go and where we were going."

It's a simple 5-step framework that's robust enough to make an $8 billion-dollar decision.

--*-*-*

"WITHOUT A COMPASS BEARING, A SHIP WOULD NEITHER FIND ITS PORT NOR BE ABLE TO ESTIMATE THE TIME REQUIRED TO GET THERE"

PETER DRUCKER

--*-*-*

Business Strategy No. 15
BLUE OCEAN STRATEGY

Introduction:

Blue Ocean Strategy was developed by globally pre-eminent management thinkers Chan Kim and Renée Mauborgne in 2005. They observed that companies tend to engage in head-to-head competition in search of sustained profitable growth.

Rather than fighting toe-to-toe with your competitors for market share and shrinking profits, this strategy instead encourages businesses to seek out uncontested market space that they can have all to their own. When successful in this pursuit, it is possible to dramatically increase the value of a company while simultaneously making the previously identified competition irrelevant.

A '**Blue Ocean**', is basically uncharted territory in the business world. You can think of Blue Ocean as: **"A market space that has yet to have been explored by any other business – meaning it is a land full of opportunity."**

If you can manage to get your company into a blue ocean in the market, you will have all the opportunity in the world to make large amounts of money in a potentially short period of time.

While that blue ocean might not remain open forever (in fact, it certainly won't remain open forever), you can make huge gains in both revenue and brand recognition while you are the only player in the game. Even as other competitors begin to work their way in, turning that "blue" ocean "red" (with competition), you should still have the advantage as you were the innovator in this space.

What are Red Oceans?

"Red Oceans" as those businesses which already contain a high level of competition. Here companies try to outperform their rivals to grab a greater share of product or service demand. As the market space gets crowded, prospects for profits and growth are reduced. Products become commodities or niche, and cutthroat competition turns the ocean bloody; hence, the term "**red oceans**".

RED OCEAN	BLUE OCEAN
"Defend Current Position" Perspective	*"Innovate & Pursue New Opportunities"* Perspective
Compete in existing market space	Create uncontested market space
Beat the competition	Make the competition irrelevant
Exploit existing demand	Create and capture new demand
Make the value-cost trade-off	Break the value-cost trade-off
Align the whole system of a firm's activities with its strategic choice of differentiation or low cost	Align the whole system of a firm's activities in pursuit of differentiation and low cost

Why you should avoid Red Oceans?

Although there is an inevitability to having to compete in crowded markets, there are too many advantages to avoiding this situation to ignore the possibility of looking for blue space. In an already contested market, there is a natural cap in place on the potential of your business. You won't be able to 'hit the jackpot' in terms of business growth or sales figures, because the market is already set.

Even if you are able to carve out a respectable share of business for yourself, it is highly unlikely that you will rocket to the top of the business world in an already competitive space. The prices and profit margins are largely set before you even arrive, meaning your ceiling is relatively low.

You can't afford to completely stay away from red oceans because that is where the majority of business takes place, but continuing to look for blue oceans is a great way to take the limit off of what you can accomplish.

Creating New Demand

Most businesses start with the idea of filling a demand in the market, but the Blue Ocean Strategy holds that it is far better to create a new demand that doesn't even exist at the moment. While doing so is obviously a great challenge, the rewards can be many.

There are new markets being created all the time by the innovation of new products and services, and the businesses that are on the cutting edge of these markets tend to be some of the largest in the world. Organizations willing to go into untested territories are taking a big gamble, but that gamble sometimes pays off in a huge way.

Finding Open Space

Of course, locating the opportunity to create a blue ocean for your business

is going to be the biggest challenge of all. It is easy to sit back and think that 'everything has already been done', even though that is clearly not the case.

There are four points to look for blue oceans around the edges of your business market.

1. **Raise.** The first point has to do with raising the quality of one factor or another as compared to industry standard. In other words, you could create a blue ocean by offering a product that is of a significantly higher quality than anything else currently offered within the industry. Perhaps you will use more advanced technology, or better materials, to develop an amazing product that grabs the attention of consumers.

By rising above and establishing a new level, you will be playing in a market all your own.

2. **Eliminate.** Many industries have barriers or characteristics that simply do not need to be in place. Often, these are issues that were once relevant, but are no longer a problem thanks to developments in technology. If you can eliminate unnecessary parts of the business tool within your organization, you could find a way into an open space that leaves you competing at a low price or on a faster timeline.

3. **Reduce.** This is the opposite of the idea of raising the level of a product or service within the industry that you compete. Instead, you can choose to reduce the standard on a point that isn't necessary in order to leave your customers with a quality item. You might be over-engineering a certain element of your product, or you may be using an expensive material where a cheaper alternative would do the same thing.

4. **Create.** The last point on the list is where innovation comes into the picture. This point has you and your company creating something that has simply never before been seen in the industry. This is probably the most difficult point to be successful with, as it takes incredible creativity and a

willingness to go out on a limb, but it also holds the biggest potential for success if your product is a hit.

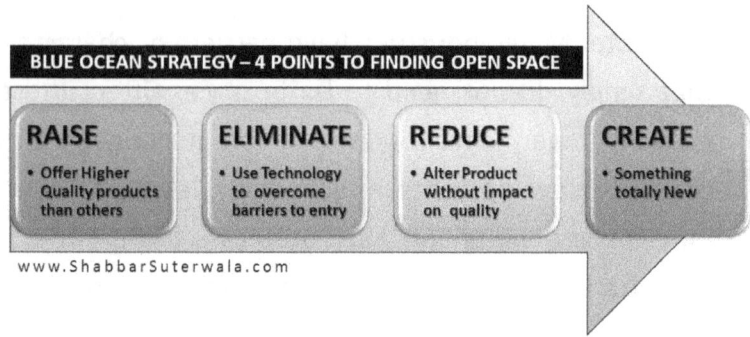

The Blue Ocean Strategy allows business owners to 'think big'. You aren't just trying to scrape by when you use this kind of strategy in your business. Instead, you are trying to achieve great things on a large scale.

It can be intimidating to approach your business from this big picture perspective, but it is exciting at the same time. If you do manage to find a section of blue ocean that you can claim as your own, it just might go down as the leading accomplishment of your professional career.

8 Key Points of Blue Ocean Strategy

1. **It's grounded in data**: Blue ocean strategy, developed by W. Chan Kim and Renée Mauborgne, is based on a decade-long study of more than 150 strategic moves spanning more than 30 industries over 100 years.

2. **It pursues differentiation and low cost**: Blue ocean strategy is based on the simultaneous pursuit of differentiation and low cost. It is an 'and-and,' not an 'either-or' strategy.

3. **It creates uncontested market space**: Blue ocean strategy doesn't aim to out-perform the competition. It aims to make the competition irrelevant by reconstructing industry boundaries.

4. **It empowers you through tools and frameworks**: Blue ocean strategy offers systematic tools and frameworks to break away from the competition and create a blue ocean of uncontested market space.

5. **It provides a step-by-step process**: From assessing the current state of play in an industry, to exploring the six paths to new market space, to understanding how to convert noncustomers into customers. Blue ocean strategy provides a clear four-step process to create your to-be blue ocean strategy.

6. **It maximizes opportunity while minimizing risk**: The blue ocean idea index allows you to test the commercial viability of your ideas and shows you how to refine your ideas to maximize your upside while minimizing downside risk.

7. **It builds execution into strategy**: The process and tools are inclusive, easy to understand and communicate, and visual – all of which makes the process non-intimidating and an effective path to building execution into strategy and the collective wisdom of a company.

8. **It shows you how to create a win-win outcome**: As an integrated approach to strategy, blue ocean strategy shows how to align the three strategy propositions – **value, profit, and people** – to ensure your organization is aligned around your new strategy and that it creates a win for buyers, the company, and for employees and stakeholders.

Popular Examples of Blue Ocean Strategy

1. Starbucks

Starbucks is a prime example of a company that implemented the Blue Ocean Strategy successfully.

There were many coffee shops that were more established when Starbucks came on the scene. Instead of focusing on their coffee, however, they worked to brand Starbucks as something different, reaching an untapped level of consumers.

The most important thing they offered was variety. They offered coffee, but they also offered teas, smoothies, and Frappuccino. They also sold CDs and newspapers, encouraging coffee lovers to stay around and chat.

This allowed Starbucks to become a social venue as well. Rather than staff their shops with rank-and-file fast food employees, they hired professional baristas, who were trained in their specialty coffee drinks. This gave the experience an air of artistry and professionalism that helped Starbucks attain "brand aspiration."

2. Flipkart.com

Flipkart was the first e-commerce website in India when popularity of internet increased and changed the shopping experience.

3. Naukri.com

Naukri.com which was founded by Sanjeev Bikhchandani. Considering the platform and time of birth of Naukri, Mr. Sanjeev had many other options to do or start-up with and enter into the competition world. But Naukri was a way different stuff. Naukri.com was found on 1997 – days which internet wasn't that popular in India. Naukri.com entered the uncontested market space with a different business strategy of that time and we all know the status now!

--*-*-*

"IT'S NOT ABOUT IDEAS. IT'S ABOUT MAKING IDEAS HAPPEN."

SCOTT BELSKY

--*-*-*

Business Strategy No. 16
DEMING'S 5 DISEASES OF MANAGEMENT

Introduction:

William Edwards Deming (1900-1993) is widely acknowledged as the leading management thinker in the field of quality. He was a statistician and business consultant whose methods helped hasten Japan's recovery after the Second World War and beyond. He derived the first philosophy and method that allowed individuals and organizations to

"Without data you're just another person with an opinion"
(W. Edwards Deming – Data Scientist)

plan and continually improve themselves, their relationships, processes, products and services. His philosophy is one of cooperation and continual improvement; it avoids blame and redefines mistakes as opportunities for improvement. Dr. Deming: The American who taught the Japanese about Quality. A household name in Japan, became the prime catalyst behind the incredible success of Japanese industry.

Background for Deming's Five Diseases of Management

Good management is at the heart of successful business. It is the management team that is going to make the decisions, which will either allow the company to thrive, or cause it to struggle, in the weeks, months, and years ahead. Do managers in your organization always seem to be leaving? Does your company frequently launch new initiatives before existing ones have settled in? Or, does it seem to focus too much on short-term profits, rather than on long-term success? If you don't address issues such as these, they can seriously damage your business.

The Deming's Five Diseases of Management

Five common problems that can prevent organizations from succeeding in the long term.

1. Lack of Consistent Purpose

One of the common mistakes made by management is not clearly understanding exactly what it is they are in business for in the first place. Without a clear purpose and goal for the future, short-term thinking tends to get in the way of long-term planning.

Many organizations never make it to the long term because they have lacked the vision to plan for what that future would hold. Every organization needs to have a very clear understanding of what it is trying to do and how it is trying to do it in order to succeed over time. When management is guided by the vision that is in place, they can make wise decisions, which will benefit both the short and long term sufficiently.

2. Emphasis on Short Term Profits

This point fits nicely in with the previous point. When choices are made only based on how to maximize short term profits – perhaps with the goal of satisfying shareholders – the long-term health of the company is compromised.

Doing things like improving the quality of products, or offering better service, don't always show up in the quarterly reports on profit and loss. Therefore, those investments that would be likely to help the company in the long run, are frequently neglected, and the books are made to look as good as they can look for right now.

The temporary profits might be nice, but they are no way to build a powerful and long-lasting organization. In the end, the emphasis on short-term profits is sure to become a drag on the business, and the profits that were once realized will likely be lost.

3. Annual Rating of Performance

Annual ratings of the staff that works underneath the upper management tend to have a devastating effect on an organization. For one thing, the employees within the company come to fear these reviews, and that fear can negatively impact their work throughout the year.

Instead of making decisions and taking actions that are best for the company, employees are forced to look out for their own self-interests by going things that will review well when the time comes.

Perhaps the biggest negative affect of the annual rating system is the loss of teamwork that is experienced. People are rarely encouraged to work together under this kind of system, for fear that someone else is going to get credit for the work that they have done.

Motivation through fear of the annual review is a lousy way to get people to work hard, and they will rarely work for the common good as a result. Again, this is another management mistake that values short-term thinking over the long-term benefit of the organization. Short-term actions might look good on a review, but they likely aren't going to take the company to new heights moving forward.

4. Mobility of Management

Consistency among the management team is something that is highly desirable, but sadly, is frequently hard to find. For companies that have trouble with management, it is very likely that the management team has not been working within the company for long.

Making smart decisions requires a deep understanding of the business that cannot be gained through textbooks or case studies. The organizations who receive the best results from their management team tend to be those who keep managers around for as long as possible, and those who don't reward those managers only for short term progress.

Again, this is another place where annual reviews and other similar systems can create trouble. A poor review may cause an otherwise talented and experienced manager to look for another job – meaning the company will lose all of their knowledge when they walk out the door.

5. Use of Visible Figures Only

The last 'disease' on the list relates to basing the decisions within the company only on measurable statistics. If it can't be seen on a balance sheet, or in a stock price, it is often ignored and this is a mistake.

Yet again, it is a mistake that is based on the short term rather than the long term. Choosing to operate in a way that only serves the needs of the profit and loss statement might make ownership or shareholders happy for now, but that happiness will fade down the line.

Some things that aren't measurable, such as positive customer service, can create long term benefits that might not be seen in the here and now.

Avoiding the five diseases listed above is not going to be easy, but it is important for the health and success of the organization in the long term. An experienced management team will understand the need to keep an eye on the long-term future rather than simply the short-term results that show up on things like quarterly reports.

With a combination of a steady management team and an eye for the future of the business, it is possible to steer clear of these pitfalls on the way to a prosperous outcome.

Deming - 14 Points of Management	
1. Create constancy of purpose 2. Adapt the new philosophy 3. Cease inspection, require evidence 4. Improve the quality of supplies 5. Continuously improve production 6. Train and educate all employees 7. Supervisor must help people	8. Drive out fear 9. Eliminate boundaries 10. Eliminate the use of slogans 11. Eliminate numerical standards 12. Let people be proud of their work 13. Encourage self-improvement 14. Commit to ever-improving quality
"94% of problems in business are systems driven and only 6% are people driven."	

Business Strategy No. 17
THE CONGRUENCE MODEL

Introduction:

The Congruence Model was first developed by David A Nadler and M L Tushman in the early 1980's. It is a useful business tool to identify what's going wrong within an organization and to identify how to fix it.

The model is based on the principle that performance stems from the following four elements: **tasks, people, structure, and culture**. The higher the congruence, or compatibility, amongst these elements, the greater the performance.

For example, if you have brilliant people working for you, but your organization's culture is not a good fit for the way they work, their brilliance will not shine through. Likewise, you can have the latest technology and superbly streamlined processes to support decision making, but if the organizational culture is highly bureaucratic, decisions will undoubtedly still get caught in the dilemma.

In order to be able to effectively change an incongruent organization to a congruent one the first step is to understand the components and how they relate to each other:

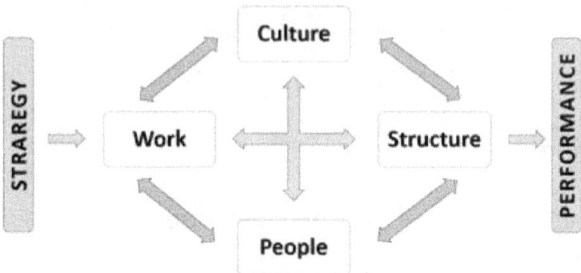

1. **Work**: What is the nature of the tasks to be performed? What are the anticipated workflows? What knowledge / skills do the tasks demand? What are the associated rewards and risks with the tasks?

2. **People:** It is important to identify the main characteristics of the people tasked to complete the core work. What knowledge / skills do they bring? What are their needs / preferences with regard to compensation (financial and non-financial)? What is the demographic of the workforce and how does this relate to their work?

3. **Structure:** This encompasses not only the formal structure, but also the systems and processes each organization creates in order to co-ordinate activity to achieve its strategy. How is the company organized? How is work measured?

4. **Culture: The informal structure of the organization.** What are the organization's norms in turns of behaviour, values,

and beliefs? What is the leadership style of the organization? How does information flow around an organization?

Once an understanding of the organization's components and their impact of performance has been gained then an organization must analyze how these elements interrelate in the entity.

1. **Work/Tasks:** You can look at your company to make sure that all the tasks you perform align with company objectives. You may find some discrepancies. For example, if your objective is to increase sales and your sales department is cutting back on payroll, you have a conflict. On the other hand, if your company objective is to introduce new products and you beef up your research and development department to have it create and improve products, your tasks are aligned with your objectives.

2. **People/Employees:** Your employees are part of the congruence of your company approach. For example, a company focused on innovation needs forward-thinking employees. If your company's main goal is to preserve existing markets, you will need employees who think conservatively. On the other hand, a company that seeks growth will want employees who can be aggressive in increasing sales and productivity.

3. **Structure/Formal Organization:** Rather than simply modeling your company after other companies, you can establish company structure and create a consistency between what you do and how you do it. For example, if you have several regional markets you service, a hierarchical structure where decisions come from the top executives at the home office may not work best for you. You might consider a modular structure, where regional managers have authority to make business decisions based on their knowledge of how to best serve their customers. Similarly, if your business requires agility to adjust to quickly changing market conditions, a structure that requires multiple managerial meetings for decisions could slow you down and hurt your ability to adjust in time.

4. **Culture/Informal Organization:** Another element of a congruence model for a business is the culture or personality your company has. If your company is aggressive, innovative and highly competitive, you will need to engage in business practices that offer opportunities to break through barriers and achieve difficult objectives. If your company is more laid-back, seeking steady but slow growth and emphasizing the quality of life among employees as much as the quality of your goods and services, you will need to guide your business so it consistently pursues opportunities that don't disrupt your pursuit of gradual improvement.

How to Use the Congruence Model

To apply the Congruence Model, start by looking at each component individually and then compare and analyze how they relate to one another.

1. ## Analyze Each Key Element Separately
    - **Tasks**: First you need to understand what work is at the core of your organization's performance. Here you are looking at the critical tasks that are done within the organization from two perspectives: What work is done, and how is it processed.
        - ➢ Does the work require specific knowledge or skill?
        - ➢ What are the intrinsic rewards involved in completing the work?
        - ➢ Is it mechanistic or creative?
        - ➢ How does the work flow?
        - ➢ What sort of approach is needed to do this work best? Quick? Thorough? Caring? Analytical? Precise? Enthusiastic?
        - ➢ Where are the interdependencies?
    - **People**: You know what work is done; now you have to look at who does it. You need to know what types of people are currently performing the organization's critical tasks.
        - ➢ Who interacts to get the work done? Bosses, employees, peers, external stakeholders.

- What skills do the people possess? Knowledge, experience, education, competencies.
- Is there a demographic profile? Age, gender, ethnicity.
- What are these people's preferences and expectations for compensation, reward, career progression, recognition, and organizational commitment?

- **Structure**: This element involves looking at the formal structure, systems and processes that support the organization.
  - How is the company organized? Mechanistic or organic.
  - Are there distinct business units or other separations? Regional, functional, by product, by market.
  - How distinct and/or rigid are the lines of authority?
  - How standardized is the work? Rules, policies, procedures.
  - How is work measured and incentivized and rewarded?

- **Culture**: Here you are concerned with the unwritten rules that define how work is really done – which depends on attitudes, beliefs, commitment, motivation and so on, as well as the formal elements of process and structure that you have already examined. This element is the hardest to define, and often the one with the most influence.

- ➢ What do people really do to get work done?
- ➢ How does information flow around the organization?
- ➢ What are the beliefs and values of individuals in the organization?
- ➢ What leadership style is adopted?
- ➢ Is there a political network in play?

2. Analyze How These Elements Interrelate in Your Organization

- • Once you have identified the major factors in performance for each of the four key elements, you need to look at how they interrelate. You are looking for areas of congruence and incongruence.
  - ➢ **Work and People**: Is the work being done by the right people?
  - ➢ **Work and Structure: Is the work done in a well-coordinated manner given the organizational structure in place?**
  - ➢ **Structure and People: Does the formal organization structure allow the people to work together effectively?**
  - ➢ **People and Culture: Are the people working within a culture that best suits them?**

> **Culture and Work: Does the culture support the nature of the work that needs to be done?**
> **Structure and Culture: Do the formal and informal structures work cooperatively or do they compete?**

3. **Step Three: Plan to Create and Maintain Congruence**

- Work through the areas of congruence and incongruence you have identified, and decide what needs to be done to resolve major incongruence and to reinforce congruence.

- As you move forward with your plan, strategy, or decision, it's important to remember that you keep on looking for the things that are well-coordinated, as well as the things that aren't.

- It's just as important to reinforce what is currently congruent, as well as change what's incongruent, and build in processes to ensure that the current congruence is maintained.

Business Strategy No. 18
THE 4 + 1 VIEW MODEL

Introduction:

The 4 + 1 View Model is a predefined set of views for organizing the design and architecture of a system. It was developed in 1995 by Philippe Kruchten, formerly the Director of Process Development at Rational Software.

The 4 + 1 View Model gets its name from the 4 primary views and 1 supporting view that are used to capture and communicate different aspects of the system.

There is an old expression that says there are two sides to every story and, there is more than one way to look at every story – different view-points to be taken. This is the idea behind the 4 +1 View Model – that there are many ways to look at something, each with a different perspective and insight than the other.

It is a mistake to look at something from only one view, as you are bound to miss aspects of it that you would have seen from other angles. If you are a manager or leader within your business, you owe it to yourself and to your team to take as many views as possible throughout the course of a project.

As the name gives away, there are four views that are covered in this model for you to consider. While the model is often used as a guideline for computer programmers and others in the IT world, it has applications to management and leadership as well.

The Four Primary View are:

1. Logical View
2. Process View
3. Development View
4. Physical View

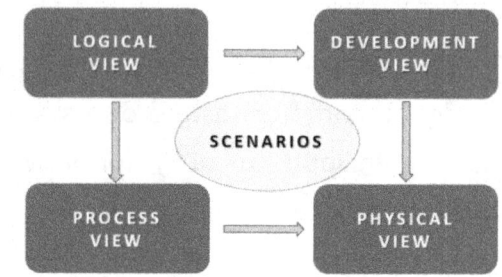

By understanding each of these views and how they play together, you can improve your own performance as a leader and get the most out of your team. Let's take a closer look at each of these four views.

1. Logical View

Taking a logical view of any system within your business is to step back and see it from a higher perspective than you normally take. The logical view can be highly beneficial to a manager who spends most of their time right in the middle of the action and rarely steps back to see how the overall picture is coming together. It is very easy to become so absorbed within the daily activities of your business that you never really think logically about what is going on.

It is also helpful, to the extent that it is possible, to put away your technical knowledge within the field and try to look at the situation from a layman's perspective.

- What would you think about the operations of the business if you had no training whatsoever?
- How would you feel about the way the organization is being run?

Technical knowledge is usually required for success, but it can also be a serious roadblock along the way. Try removing yourself from what you know and just think about the situation logically as if it were a field you knew nothing about. This can be a powerful perspective to take, and could lead you to making some serious changes.

2. Process View

This is basically the other side of the coin from the logical view. With the process view, you want to get in 'deep' to the day-to-day operations and think critically about how they work and if they work. What could be changed to improve performance, or is the system already running optimally?

Process view has a lot to do with how employees work together, and what those interactions say about the organization as a whole. Depending on how you choose to manage your employees, this view could be the most revealing of them all.

It is important not to take shortcuts when trying to get a clear picture of the organization through the process view. You really need to understand every last detail and how all of the various inputs connect with one another. Knowing the daily operation of the business as closely as possible is a great advantage when it comes to decision making because you will be better able to predict problems and challenges that could arise from changes that are made.

3. Development View

Business is all about developing new ideas and making sure that you don't become stuck in a rut doing the same old thing. Taking a developmental view of your business is helpful in order to generate new ideas and maybe shed light on old ideas that never quite made it to market.

- **The development of your business or organization is not going to happen on its own – you are going to need to make it happen through critical thinking and constant analysis.**

Also, it likely won't be good enough to have only one or two people taking a developmental view. Rather, everyone within the organization should be tasked with thinking this way, and they should have the freedom to express new ideas and point toward opportunities.

Getting the most from your employees' means empowering them to think for themselves and offer up new ideas and directions that could potentially power the organization into the future.

4. Physical View

It might be best to think of this view as a 'state of the union' analysis. You will want to look at the organization as a whole, as it is right now. Not in relation to future goals or opportunities that may come along – but what it is at this point in time.

This realistic view of the organization should give you a reality check in terms of what your strengths and weaknesses really are, and what you can do to improve on them or take advantage of them. Many businesses choose to not see the bad things for fear of what they might find. If you want to win over your competition, you have to be willing to look at things that might not be so pretty in order to correct them.

The + 1 Supporting view or also known as Scenario / Use case View

This view describes the functionality of the system from the perspective of external actors. Putting it all together and Evaluating and Validating to show the design is complete.

Why is it called the 4 + 1 instead of just 5?

The use case view has a special significance. When all other views are finished, its effectively redundant. However, all other views would not be possible without it. It details the high levels requirements of the system. The other views detail how those requirements are realized.

Use of the 4 + 1 View Model

It makes modeling easier. Better organization with better separation of concern. The 4 + 1 approach provides a way for architects to be able to prioritize modeling concerns. The 4 + 1 approach makes it possible for stakeholders to get the parts of the model that are relevant to them.

While the 4 +1 View Model is more commonly referenced when it comes to software development and engineering, the principles certainly apply directly to the operation of any organization. It is always healthy to take a fresh perspective and see what you can find out about your company when you look at it from as many different angles as possible.

Work your way through the four views on this list to make sure that you are missing threats or opportunities that might be right under your nose. Make sure that you and the rest of your team are using this model to drive the way you think about business.

Summary

The 4 +1 model has its origins in software engineering but it can also be used outside of that discipline.

1. The **logical view** is where the overall structure of the application is conveyed. Another way to characterize the logical view is to think of it as the interfaces to the environment in the most general of contexts.
2. The **process view** is used to paint a picture describing the underlying processes and tasks, which are occurring within the system, as well as the channels of communication between them. The interrelationships amongst processes should be visible as well as the synchronization mechanisms.
3. The **development view** provides perspective on the software's organization. The components of the system as well as their inter dependencies are outlined within this view.
4. The **physical view** is used to describe the hardware and software setup that is required by the system. In this view we gain an appreciation of how the hardware and software components are combined to form the deployed product.
5. Use **Case View**: this view describes the functionality of the system from the perspective of external actors.

--*-*-*

"AN ENTREPRENEUR ISN'T

SOMEONE WHO OWNS A BUSINESS.

IT'S SOMEONE WHOM MAKES

THINGS HAPPEN"

TIM FERRISS

--*-*-*

Business Strategy No. 19

KAY'S DISTINCTIVE CAPABILITIES FRAMEWORK

Introduction:

John Kay, economics professor at London Business School, developed the Distinctive Capabilities Framework and wrote about it in his 1993 "Foundations of Corporate Success."

You might find it hard to feel **"distinctive"** in the business world. After all, there is an incredible amount of competition in nearly every market, and it seems that all of the good ideas have either been used already, or they have been copied as soon as they hit the market. A company cannot achieve success in the long run only by:

- coming up with better products or services,
- making the selling process more effective or
- by implementing better methods than their rivals.

So how can you stand out and rise above the competition when there is so much market saturation already in place? Key's Distinctive Capabilities Framework is a great place to start when thinking about just such as problem. In order to achieve success, a company should implement at least one of the three capabilities mentioned by Kay.

What is Distinctive Capabilities Framework?

Distinctive Capabilities Framework are capabilities that are unique to your business, which give you a competitive advantage over the rest of the market. All business owners and managers understand that they need a unique selling proposition, or USP, in order to make a dent in a competitive market.

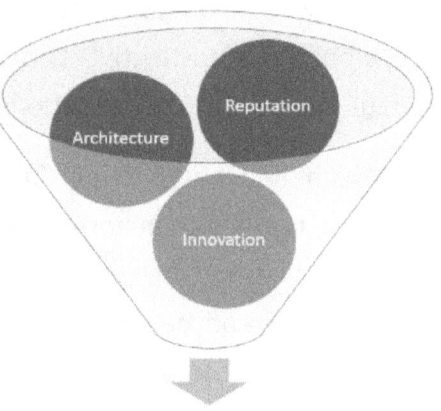

However, that USP can be hard to find, unless you have the advantage of leveraging one or more

Distinctive Capabilities Framework

distinctive capabilities that are held by your company. While a distinctive capability is not, in and of itself, a competitive advantage, it is what gives you the opportunity to create a competitive advantage that can be taken to market.

Think about distinctive capabilities in the same way you would think about talent for an individual – it is a differentiating factor, and it provides the opportunity to succeed down the road.

The Three Distinctive Capabilities

Distinctive capabilities need to be, by definition, things that remain unique to the company over the long haul. Only then will they truly be advantages, and only then will they be able to lead the business to success.

According to Kay, true distinctive capabilities fall into one of three categories. Those categories are listed below, along with a quick definition.

1. **Reputation**
   - You probably already make many of your buying decisions on a day to day basis on the foundation of reputation, so there should be no doubt in your mind that this is a powerful distinctive capability.
   - If you can build a brand reputation that evokes feelings of trust and confidence in the consumer, you have already won the battle.
   - It is not easy to develop a positive reputation for your brand, but when you do, that reputation should be treated like gold because it is an incredibly valuable commodity.
   - A good reputation can rise above everything else to make the buying decision easy for the consumer. Rather than picking an item based on cost or marketing, the buyer may select your product on the strength of your reputation alone – which is a unique competitive advantage that cannot be easily replicated by your competition.

- Although they may be able to create a product that is similar, or

  even identical, to what you offer, the competition cannot take your

  brand name, and it is that brand that contains a great deal of your

  distinctive capability.

2. Architecture

- The structure of your business is unique, and can therefore become a distinctive capability when it is formed in such 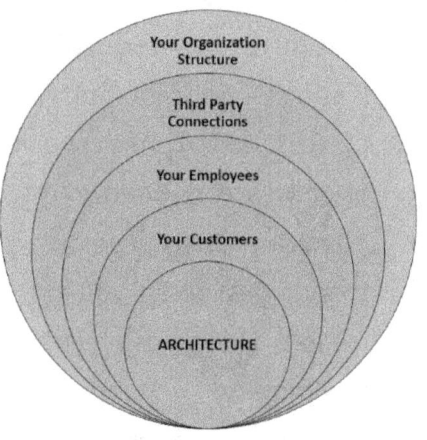 a way that it provides value to the business.

- The connections you have with suppliers, the people you have working for the company, the list of customers that you have accumulated to this point, all of those groups come together to form the architecture of your business.

- There is going to be some overlap with your competition on these points, specifically with regard to customers and suppliers, but the specific structure of your organization is still going to be unique. Taking the time to build this part of the business with great care could lead you to having a big competitive advantage in the marketplace.

3. **Innovation**
   - It is often the most innovative companies who are proven to be the most successful in the long run. Why is that? Because they can remain one or two steps ahead of the competition on an ongoing basis.
   - The products that they innovate may not remain unique for long, because there will always be competition doing what it can to copy the successful products that are on the market, but that is okay because an innovative company is always moving on to the next big thing.
   - By consistently innovating with new products and ideas, you can leave your competition struggling to keep up.
   - Another benefit of innovating is building up your reputation as was mentioned in the first capability. When consumers realize that you are consistently innovating within your field, you may build up a degree of brand loyalty and trust that can carry you to a large market share.

- Even when other 'copycat' products hit the shelves, you may still come out on top because of your reputation as an innovator in the industry.

Using Kay's Distinctive Capabilities Framework will allow you to think about your business in a way that may be new and revealing. Work through the three capabilities that are defined in this framework to find where you might be able to stand out from the competition.

The sooner you figure out what it is that makes your company unique from the rest of the field, the sooner you can exploit those differences to claim a bigger share of the market.

In order to achieve success, a company should implement at least one of the three distinctive capabilities mentioned by Kay.

- The buyer may select your product on the strength of your reputation alone – which is a unique competitive advantage that cannot be easily replicated by your competition.
- Architecture is the connections you have with suppliers, the people you have working for the company, and the list of customers that you have accumulated.
- The most innovative companies are often the most successful in the long run because they can remain ahead of the competition on an ongoing basis.

A company can use any or all of these distinctive capabilities to be consistently successful.

Example:

McDonald's and Baba Ramdev's Patanjali are classical uses its distinctive competency of effective control systems to earn high profits from its franchises.

--*-*-*

"WITHOUT STRATEGY, EXECUTION IS
AIMLESS. WITHOUT EXECUTION,
STRATEGY IS USELESS."

MORRIS CHANG

--*-*-*

Business Strategy No. 20
NET PROMOTER SCORE

Introduction:

Net Promoter Score (NPS) has become a buzzword in business in the last few years, and is widely used in finding Customer Loyalty by Business Owners

What is Net Promoter Score (NPS)?

Net Promoter Score (NPS) is a management tool that can be used to gauge the loyalty of a firm's customer relationships. It serves as an alternative to traditional customer satisfaction research and is claimed to be correlated with revenue growth.

NPS is data gathered by getting responses from your Customer by asking a **"Single Question"**.

For Example:

"How likely is it that you would recommend our company / product / service to a friend or colleague?" **(Give your Score between 10 and 1)**

"10 being Very Likely" all the way to "0 being Not at all Likely"

- Score between 0 to 6 are called **"DETRACTORS"**
- Score of 7 or 8 are called **"PASSIVE"**
- Score of 9 or 10 are called **"PROMOTERS"**

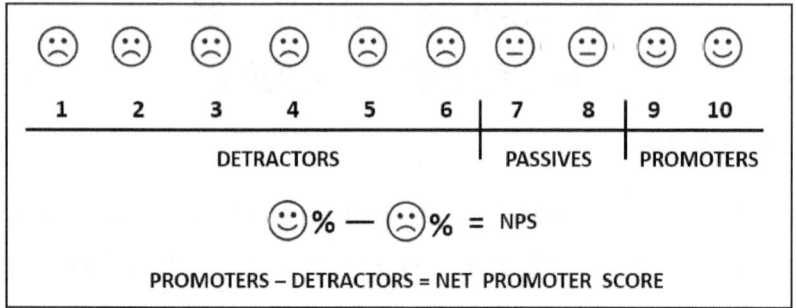

How to Calculate the Responses? (The Formula)

Imagine that 25% of customers gave you a score of 9 and 10 (Promoters), while 15% gave a score between 0 and 6 (Detractors). Your NPS would be +10 (25 -15 = 10).

Benefits and Uses of NPS

- One of the biggest benefits of the NPS is that it's simple to use.
- With one question, you can objectively measure customer loyalty, and gauge how that loyalty will affect future growth.
- Its greatest strength is the simplicity, making it functional and interpretable for every stakeholder.
- You can then use your NPS as a benchmark to measure changes in your customer service.

How does NPS Helps in Business?

- Considering the large number of big companies using this tool on a continuous basis, it certainly has proven its worth.

- The Net Promoter Score helps you serve your current customers better. For example, if your score is negative, it shows that you may be better off spending money on improving customer service rather than advertising to bring new customers on board.

- NPS is only a **starting point**. After the analysis, the real work can begin: improving the organization and taking actions to boost the NPS.

- NPS allows you to perfectly assess at which stage your organization is in this growth process.

Make Action Plan for Applying each Strategies in your Business

Strategy No	Read on (Date)	What will I Do / When / Where / How
1		
2		
3		
4		
5		
6		
7		
8		
9		
10		
11		
12		
13		
14		
15		
16		
17		
18		
19		
20